Spain From a Backpack

Edited by
Mark Pearson and Martin Westerman

Europe From a Backpack
www.europebackpack.com

SPAIN FROM A BACKPACK.
Copyright © 2006 by Pearson Venture Group.
All rights reserved. Printed in the United States of America.

No part of this book may be used or reproduced
in any manner whatsoever without written permission
except in the case of brief quotations embodied
in critical articles and reviews. Photos are used
by permission and are the property
of the original copyright holders.

Requests for permission should be addressed to:
Pearson Venture Group
P.O. Box 70525
Seattle, WA 98127-0525
U.S.A.

For more information, visit www.EuropeBackpack.com

Cover design and graphics: Greg Pearson
Copy editing and page layout: Tracy Cutchlow

Library of Congress Cataloging-in-Publication Data
Pearson, Mark (Mark R), 1980—
Westerman, Martin (Martin), 1950—
Spain from a backpack. – 1st ed.
p. cm. -- (Europe From a Backpack Series)

ISBN (10): 0-9743552-5-9
ISBN (13): 978-09743552-5-2
1. Spain—Description and travel.
2. Pearson, Mark. 3. Westerman, Martin.
Library of Congress Control Number: 2006932743

*To my mom, Claire,
who travels the world but is still
a Saskatchewan farm girl at heart*

TARJETA POSTAL

For my part, I travel not to go anywhere, but to go. I travel for travel's sake. The great affair is to move.
- Robert Louis Stevenson

stories

barcelona & valencia

Tomato Fight!	25
Restless Spain	29
Bang, Bang! The Butane Man	37
City on Fire	43
No Shoes, No Shirts, No Problems	49

madrid

Close Quarters	61
Life as a Metro Musician	69
Mugged!	73
Her	81
First, *un Bocata de Calamares*	85
Off the Map	89
Robbed in the Rastro	95
Animal Instincts	101
Losing Juan	107
Talking My Way Into Spain	115

authors

garrick aden-buie	69
jon azpiri	49
evan l. balkan	89
pamela barrus	73
judy boersema	205
elliott dykes	177
mike elkin	25
nicola escario	115
nicholas gill	29
mara ginnane	149
halldór örn gunnarsson	171
lauren guza	61
elizabeth landau	213
katherine lent	231
peter j. malcolm	225
eileen mckee	141
dave munsell	81
danielle mutarelli	37
cara nissman	43
mike riley	161
salina ronderos	95
miranda runcie	187
alicia jeanien salcedo-báez	133
rachel sarah	125
christine sarkis	197
lawrence schimel	101
lauren trojniar	219
lisa d. tossey	107
jimmy vielkind	183
kip wilson	85

stories, *con't*

pamplona & the camino

Running for the Boy	125
Crazy Girl	133
The End of the World	141
To Be a Pilgrim	149

andalusia

What I Learned About *Coleoptera* By Having a Few Climb Up My Shorts	161
Miguel's Bar	171
Spain Without a Backpack	177
Always Book Ahead	183
Meeting Pepe's Mom	187
Eight to a Compartment	197
Thumbs Up	205
Discovering My *Duende*	213
A Bang-Up Job	219
The Curse of the Tasseled Loafers	225
Goodbye, Granada	231

Introduction

Welcome to Spain, the Iberian Peninsula, the 12th-century western border of the Moorish Empire, jump-off point to mysterious Africa. You hold the gateway in your hands: By opening *Spain From a Backpack*, you are transporting yourself for the next marvelous moments to the España of blocky Basque castles, intricate Moorish designs and fanciful Gaudi creations. And welcome to a different pace of life—a pace informed by centuries of artful and bloody history, where we rise and start work early, siesta in the afternoon, and stay up late. We shop for our food every few days in open-air markets, for olives and tapenade, crusty breads, cheeses, meats, fresh tomatoes and garlic, and we cook for the joy of it. We go out for tapas in the evening, then dine in leisure, never bothered by waiters repeatedly asking, "May I take your plate?"

This is how our book series started: My co-editor, Mark Pearson, observed lots of Europe guidebooks on the market, all explaining where to go and what to do, but few books that tell what it's like to actually *be* in Europe; and virtually none written by and for backpackers. These twenty- or thirty-somethings carry their worldly possessions on their backs, traveling on a shoestring budget. Backpackers decide each day where they will go and what they will do, and, often, they experience marvels that elude people who carry suitcases and make reservations. Every year, nearly two million American, and hundreds of thousands of British, Canadian and Australian, backpackers are drawn to Europe for travel, study and work.

Fresh from studying in and backpacking around Europe himself, Mark put out the word for stories on the Web, and, to date, we have received more than 1,000 submissions from around the world. He approached me to edit the first collection, *Europe From a Backpack: Real Stories from Young Travelers Abroad,* and the more I read, the more I realized we had to do these books. We select the stories based on simple criteria: well-written, authentic, first-hand. And each one brings back wonderful memories for each of us.

For me, it's when I first knocked around Europe as a young man just out of the Coast Guard. I grew long hair and a beard, and hitchhiked with my buddy Craig out of London and across the continent, to end up picking oranges and grapefruit on a kibbutz in northern Israel. I started calling myself a "United Statian," because calling myself an "American" seemed presumptuous, since everybody else from every other country in our hemisphere is American, too. These were months of new tastes and aromas, surprising characters, awesome horizons, adventures and discoveries; of exploration and growth.

Europe, the first book in our series, covered a wide range of travelers, juvenile to mature, and a wide range of subjects, simple to complex:

the Berlin art scene, life and death on a Scottish farm at lambing season, and finding love again as a couple in Budapest. One was a serious art student seeking the right color for sky blue, for a painting class near the Eiffel Tower, when a despondent Frenchman jumped off its top. Others were party animals and thrill seekers (one snuck into the Roman Colosseum in one story, and flipped his Spanish rental car in another). Some just wanted comfort for their homesickness, as did the student who discovered an all-American Christmas in snowbound Lublijana, Slovenia.

Now, in this second book of our series, *Spain From a Backpack*, we meet a fresh group of young writers who take us through the flavors and characters of Iberia. They follow in the footsteps of Hemingway—running with the bulls in Pamplona, drinking local wine, fighting a war in Buñol (well, for an hour, with 90,000 pounds of tomatoes). But they also blaze their own trails.

One young woman fights through the weather and pain of the 800-kilometer Camino de Santiago pilgrimage, and transforms her life ("To Be a Pilgrim"). Two men just out for a picnic dinner in the beach dunes become the lightning rods for *coleoptera* beetles ("A Few Climb Up My Shorts").

Some come to Spain seeking ways they can integrate into the culture, and perhaps even become Spanish, through dance ("Finding My *Duende*") or family ("Meeting Pepe's Mom"). Others resist integrating ("Bang, Bang! The Butane Man") or actively fight it ("Robbed in the Rastro").

Some happen upon an appreciation of the culture by accident, in their train car ("Eight to a Compartment"); some fall in love with it and get married ("Running for the Boy"); some just poke their heads into it ("Miguel's Bar"), and some are shut out of it completely ("The Curse of the Tassled Loafers").

Overall, these stories tell us what the guidebooks don't: how to live on the ground once we arrive. We not only get the thrill of living vicariously through someone else's travels—enjoying fond memories if we have traveled, and getting inspired if we haven't—but we also learn, through the hindsight these travelers provide, wisdom about what to do and what not to do when we actually get there. The book serves as a tantalizing foretaste of what awaits us, and as an escape from our daily lives; a refreshing break from the ordinary.

As one of our readers noted, "This collection should inspire any traveler to record their memories in a journal. A few unforgettable travel anecdotes are far superior to a collection of a hundred photo slides to torture your friends and family with."

Since the dawn of humans, we have loved good stories. So, we invite you to turn the page and indulge in this treasure trove of tales you've discovered.

Martin Westerman
www.europebackpack.com

The traveler sees what he sees. The tourist sees what he has come to see.
— Gilbert K. Chesterton

Barcelona & Valencia

Buñol

Tomato Fight!

mike elkin

Whether the Americans to my right said "tomayto" or the Brits to my left said "tomahto," what mattered was throwing as many tomatoes as possible. Behold *La Tomatina*, a gladiatorial tomato food fight in the village of Buñol. It's a vegetarian warrior's dream.

Imagine a junior-high cafeteria food fight. Now imagine the entire junior-high class participating in the food fight. Now imagine everyone from the elementary and high schools pitching in, too. Now imagine being outside, and that everything on the tables, from the sloppy joes to the foot-long hot dogs, is tomatoes. As the cliché goes, the streets ran red that day.

I had been traveling through Andalusia when a friend in Madrid invited me to join his gang heading to Buñol, about 20 miles west of Valencia. The tomato fight there takes place annually, on the last Wednesday of August. My instructions were to bring a bathing suit and shoes that I wouldn't mind destroying. Off I went.

The village was not unlike other small Spanish villages in the region: a few narrow, cobblestone streets winding around whitewashed houses baking in the summer heat. But that week, thousands of Spaniards, Brits, Germans, Americans and Japanese flocked to the village for the tomato fight and the week-long festival that had grown up around it. We arrived in Buñol the morning of the fight and eagerly joined the rank and file for a breakfast of beer and tapas. As noon approached, the masses squeezed into the tiny plaza like clowns into a car, while the locals unfurled gigantic plastic sheets from their roofs to protect the buildings' façades.

Suddenly a blast of water hit me straight on. People were spraying us with high-pressure water cannons, the kind used to remove barnacles from century-old ships, or anti-globalization protesters from international summits. Then Spaniards on rooftops began tossing buckets of water on unsuspecting people below. From 30 feet, that's no sprinkle.

An unwritten rule decreed T-shirts were not allowed. "So let me help you remove that shirt, kind sir or madam," the friendly mob would say, and proceed to tear the thing from your body. Then they'd tie the fragments of your former shirt into knots and fling the wet cloth at high speeds into the crowd. Turning my head at an inopportune moment, one caught my eye, whipping my head back like a Pez dispenser and busting a blood vessel.

I knelt down in pain. But there was no rest for me. A loud cannon shot silenced the crowd, and then the grinding of truck gears up the road ignited the atmosphere again. Six large dump trucks, bursting with soggy tomatoes, made their way into the plaza and unloaded their ammunition. Mayhem erupted as thousands of revelers snatched up tomatoes from the ground and hurled them at their neighbors. A friend gave me swimming goggles to protect me from the blinding tomato juice, but they just got caked with tomato bits. Off they came. My eyes stung, but I couldn't dwell on it—there were tomatoes to be thrown.

My instructions were to bring a bathing suit and shoes that I wouldn't mind destroying. Off I went.

Soon, more truck engines were heard over the screams and shouts. The melee stopped and the crowd parted, each side eying the other like gunfighters, just waiting for the trucks to finish unloading before unleashing another vegetable fury.

Our foes were not only the half-naked savages around us, but also local kids taunting playfully from unprotected windows. Someone would shout and point to a nearby window, and a group of us would instinctively swivel, aim and fire at the offender who was not brave enough to take to the battlefield.

On we fought, the adrenaline running faster than the tomato juice in the gutters. Most food fights last a few minutes; *La Tomatina* runs a full hour. This may not be a long time for geologists or Teamsters, but when you're wading up to your knees in reddish sludge while thousands of people chuck about 90,000 pounds of tomatoes at you, it's exhausting.

When the cannon roared again, we all dropped our tomatoes, applauded, cheered, and embraced our neighbors. I collapsed where I stood. Gradually, I staggered down the road to a wide-open space where the town had organized communal showers. Still, I was picking tomato bits from bodily crevices for weeks after.

A Spaniard told me later not to bother. By the time I finished cleaning myself, he said, it would be time for another *Tomatina*.

AFTER TRAVELING *through Western Europe in college, Mike Elkin decided to make Spain his home, working as a freelance journalist in Madrid for three years. Now on a brief break in Dublin, Mike yearns for Spanish food—even some tomatoes.*

Barcelona

Restless Spain

nicholas gill

as we pulled into Barcelona's Estación França, I picked up my new, $200, lime-green backpack, and stepped off the train with my brother and two American friends we'd met in Interlaken. It was Friday night, and people filled the streets, many walking arm in arm. Lovely olive-skinned *señoritas* kissed each other's cheeks. I was 18, just out of high school, and near the end of my European-continent trip. Wild, restless Spain had been in my thoughts for weeks.

We went from place to place looking for lodging, but we found nowhere to sleep that night in Barcelona. Someone suggested sleeping on the beach. It sounded good to me—sleeping beneath the stars, listening to the sounds of the sea, my back against the earth. No bed could provide this.

Everyone had been tense until we decided to give up looking. Lightening up, we found an outdoor café, ordered drinks, and enjoyed telling tales of coffeehouses in Amsterdam and pubs in London. I became as disoriented as I was blissful, and when the café closed, we made our way to the beach. Plenty of others had the same idea, mostly backpackers, but also some bums and junkies. There were four of us, so I didn't expect any trouble. We formed a circle and made our beds in the sand. I felt tired and more comfortable than I had in days. The night was clear and warm, and I smiled as the gentle murmur of the Mediterranean put me softly to sleep.

I awoke sensing that something was wrong. My head hurt; my sight was a little fuzzy. I wasn't sure how long I'd been out, but it couldn't have been more than an hour or two. It was still night, and everyone else was asleep. I thought I had tied myself to my pack, but I couldn't feel it. I jumped up and looked around. It was gone. I became frantic. I tried to wake everyone, but they were all passed out, too inebriated and exhausted to make sense of my ranting. I walked a circle around the camp we had set up. It was not there.

I finally woke my brother and demanded he give me his knife. I was angry, upset and fearless. I was going to get my things back from those thieves. They couldn't have gone far, I thought. I was going to find them. I ran around the beach inspecting anything I thought looked suspicious. Adrenaline was pumping through my veins. I was prepared to do whatever it took to get my possessions back, my collection of objects from a continental trek.

I approached some groups of sleeping people several times, thinking I may have missed something. I asked bums who spoke no English if they had seen my backpack. They gave me no answers. Frustrated, I found some wooden chairs on the concrete boardwalk and beat them as hard as I could against the wall, screaming. Finally, in despair, I returned to my friends. They were aware of my situation—in a hazy, dream-like sort of way—but went back to sleep. Their packs were all there. One of them was lying three feet away from its owner. *Why didn't the thieves take that one?* I thought. I sat there, disappointed, but only for a minute. I wasn't going to give up that easily. My pack was somewhere. I was going to slow down my search, and look further and more carefully than I had before. I'd spend all night if I had to.

A half-mile or so down the beach from my friends, I found a van full of policemen chatting with some people on bikes. I tried to remember some of the Spanish I had already forgotten from high school. My *macchina* was missing. No, that wasn't the word. Anyway, they speak Catalan here.

"¿*Mochila?*" one of them asked.

"Yes. *Sí*. That's it. *Mochila*," I said as I recognized

the word. "It's gone. Stolen." I raised my arms in the air to signify "missing."

I got in the van. I didn't really know what was going on. We drove around the city. They asked me questions I couldn't answer. "*Mochila* ... missing," I said, reassuring myself that they knew what I was talking about. They whistled at girls on sidewalks and laughed. I tried to laugh along with them, but I couldn't. We went to a station somewhere in the city; they sat me down on a stiff chair in a bare cement hallway and left. I waited for something to happen. The only other person in the hall was a startled old Spaniard with crutches who kept trying to talk to me. From what I could make out, he had been robbed or attacked. There were tears in his eyes.

It was the first time I began giving any thought to what was in my bag. Now I felt worse.

After what seemed like hours, a policeman who spoke some English brought me into a room to fill out a report of what exactly was missing. It was the first time I began giving any thought to what was in my bag. Now I felt worse.

Besides all of my clothes, there were souvenirs from a dozen countries: postcards, CDs, T-shirts, and various items I'd picked up along the way. My camera was gone, as were the 20 or so rolls of film I had shot. I thought of the pictures I would never be able to see: the one of me hoisting a beer with a table of Japanese students at the Hofbrauhaus; the one I took of the Sistine Chapel ceiling that almost got me thrown out. All of those memories would be lost. I was lucky enough to have kept my passport and wallet in my pockets.

I completed the form and handed it to the officer. He led me to the door outside. "Aren't you going to give me a ride?" I asked. No, they answered, they did not do that. I had no idea where I was, where on the beach my friends were, or even what time I'd left. I walked outside. The officer warned me to watch out for Arabs, saying they maced people so they could rob them. If I saw any, he said, I should run.

Scared now, I ran through the streets, looking every which way for Arabs. The knife came out of my pocket; I grasped it firmly in my hand. I wasn't going to let anything else be taken from me. I could just imagine my friends back home hearing that I died in a knife fight with an Arab in Spain.

The wind blew hard, tossing leaves and trash under the bright streetlights. I ran in circles at first, but the smell of salt in the air finally led me back to the beach. That was the easy part. Now, I had to find my friends. The beach looked the same everywhere. I ran in one direction, then, thinking I had gone too far, headed in the other. My calves ached from running in the thick sand. I felt weary and could barely stay awake, but still I ran as fast as I could. I worried that my friends had left to look for me, since I had been gone so long, and that I would never be able to find them.

I ran for miles and miles, always feeling as though I was getting nowhere—half an hour in one direction, half an hour in another, then back again. Eventually, my surroundings began to look more familiar. The place that I had left hours before was still there. In fact, my friends were still sleeping. I collapsed onto the beach and tried to go to sleep, hoping that I would wake up well-rested, next to my belongings.

But I could not fall asleep. The sky was beginning to lighten and gulls were circling above. I looked around and saw what was left of my things: a blanket, an inflatable neck cushion, and a book that I had yet to finish. I sat and watched the tide roll in. I could feel the temperature rising by the minute. Humiliated, I felt like the gulls were laughing at me. My pack was gone. I wasn't getting it back.

Slowly, I began to understand my lost things for what they were: things. Other than the photos, everything would be worn out or thrown away in the next few years. It could all be replaced. The photos I couldn't reproduce, but my memories were alive.

Tired and heartbroken, I began to laugh along with the gulls. I was disenchanted but not devastated. I looked out far across the ancient water, farther than I ever had before, and accepted the rising sun.

NICHOLAS GILL *is a freelance writer and photographer based in Columbus, Ohio. He is the author of "Adventure Guide Peru" (Hunter Publishing, 2006). After graduating from Ohio State*

University, he spent several years abroad in search of adventure. However, he and his Peruvian wife are intent on settling in the United States ... somewhere.

Barcelona

Bang, Bang! The Butane Man

danielle mutarelli

I used to think that "living abroad" meant you had an address, a job and a bank account. I had those things in Barcelona.

The address was a crummy apartment I shared with 13 other people in what used to be a brothel. The job just paid for my room. And the bank account was virtually useless, because the bank was across town and I could never seem to get there on a day that wasn't a holiday. And also I had no money.

Truth was, despite having all those things, I didn't feel like I actually lived in Barcelona. I was failing to do the one thing that enables you to truly live abroad:

adapt. I simply couldn't accept the idiosyncrasies of that gorgeous city's culture.

I resisted those tiny *tapas*, because they were just a tease. I resisted the idea that a city should shut down for at least one major holiday a week. I resisted the nightlife. (Late nights truly killed me. I pleaded with my foreign friends to go out just once before 1 a.m., but they never did, and I usually found myself in bed before "the night" had begun.)

But the thing I boycotted most was butane, which fuels the majority of kitchen ovens and water heaters in Barcelona. I'm so cautious with fire, I don't even burn candles. So you can imagine how I felt about opening up a gas valve and sticking a match to it. The whole setup terrified me, and I ended up eating a lot of cold cereal and taking many cold showers.

And obtaining butane was so archaic! You don't set up an account and have the stuff delivered to your flat on a regular basis. You don't ring up your local butane distributors and ask them to drop off a couple of tanks. No, you must seek out the butane man who peddles it on the street. He wheels his cart, piled high with tanks of explosive gas, through Barcelona's narrow, twisting alleys and side streets, alerting you to his presence by banging on the tanks with a screwdriver (is that even safe?!) and belting out, "*Buu-taaa-noooo!*"

The butane man does not adhere to any set schedule; he makes his own. His singsong and banging echo throughout the neighborhood at irregular hours on differing days, guaranteed to be the ones when you're trying to sleep off your worst hangover ever. And the moment you hear the butane man, you must dash down your stairs and race into the street, or you'll miss him 'til whatever time he next comes.

For months, I avoided these odd transactions. I contributed my butane funds to the house account, and I let my flatmates handle the rest. But one day, my landlord elected me as the butane retriever. I couldn't understand why he'd picked me. I was by far the least competent at this task of anyone in the flat, if not the entire city. For days, I pretended that I'd forgotten, hoping someone else would step up to the job. Sure, I felt like a slacker, but I assured myself: "It's not your problem. You don't use the butane."

Yet, my landlord persisted, and he asked me daily if I'd gotten the butane. It was ludicrous. It seemed as if he'd come upon selecting me by asking himself a short list of questions:

1. Q: Who repeatedly locks herself out of the flat?
   A: Dani.
2. Q: Who has caused the washer to overflow no fewer than three times?
   A: Dani.
3. Q: Who has the Spanish vocabulary of a 5-year-old, and is least likely to obtain anything other than water?
   A: Dani.

Then one day, I got a hankering for Ramen noodles. I had abused my palate in college, and nothing but Ramen noodles would suffice now. I grabbed my pot of water and snuck over to use our neighbors' stove.

Their kitchen was in a state. They had butane, yes, but they also had an ambitious trail of ants making their way in through the window, over the sink, along the edge of the cupboard, across the wall, down the door frame, and into one of three piles of trash. It took me a moment to even locate the oven beneath the mountain of crockery. But pilferers can't be choosers. I pushed the crud-encrusted pans off the range, and, holding my breath, I opened the valve, said a prayer, and lit the match. The fire flared under the pot, and I sat back and waited for the water to boil.

Truth was, I was feeling guilty. I was taking a meager amount of butane, but still, it wasn't mine. I was a thief. I just couldn't get my life in Barcelona right. I was a failure. And the root of the problem was nothing but my own resistance. I looked around the kitchen. This was the story of my life in Barcelona, I realized: I'd do anything, even steal, to avoid getting out there and living as a local. I leaned over and turned off the stove, dumped my pot of water in the sink, and walked back to my flat. It seemed destined that, right then, I would hear the butane man's clanging coming up from the street. I grabbed our flat's empty tank and headed down the stairs to meet the butane man.

His cart was loaded with orange tanks, and he

nodded as I approached. We exchanged my empty tank for one of his full ones, and the deal was done. It was so simple.

The butane man smiled at me, out of gratitude, I gathered, because he was pushing a slightly lighter load. But it was more than that. It was as if he knew that it was my first time; that I was no longer a butane virgin. The full tank was heavy, but I felt empowered as I made my way back up the stairs. After all these months in Barcelona, I felt that I was now officially living in Barcelona. I'd made the transition. Maybe this is why my landlord had selected me. Maybe meeting the butane man was a sort of Barcelona rite of passage.

> Maybe meeting the butane man was a sort of Barcelona rite of passage.

At the top of the stairs, I stood in front of our flat's door, feeling changed. Life in Barcelona suddenly didn't feel so hard. I was living abroad. I could become accustomed to these Barcelona ways. I could acclimatize. I was not such an old dog; I was not so incompetent.

Quite pleased with myself, I reached to open the door. It was locked. And, I realized, my keys were inside.

DANIELLE MUTARELLI *lived in Barcelona, teaching English and locking herself out of her apartment. The latter led her to discover that watching the sun rise over Sagrada Familia is simply awe-inspiring.*

Valencia

City on Fire

cara nissman

Saying that Valencia in March is a blast is like saying Times Square on New Year's Eve is crowded. Every March 15 to 19, this coastal Spanish city bursts with raucous noise and vibrant colors for *Las Fallas* ("The Torches"), ending in a wild final night of fireworks. After months of living in Madrid and backpacking around Spain, I had heard enough about *Las Fallas* to know I didn't want to miss it.

The Valencia version dates to the 15th century, when craftsmen took the torches used to light the city's streets during winter, and burned them in bonfires on the feast day of San José, patron saint of workers. Over the years, the day has expanded into a riotous week of bonfires, parades and fireworks explosions, celebrated by several million people.

Today, each *barrio* in the city spends up to a year building a *falla* that's 20 feet tall, and dozens of smaller *ninots* to surround it. These startlingly lifelike statues satirize current events and lampoon public figures. Meticulously built of cardboard, wood and plaster, the fantastic constructions are displayed during the week of festivities.

Then, on the last day, called *La Crema* ("The Burning"), men with axes chop holes in the figures and fill them with fireworks, to be set ablaze at midnight. At 1 a.m., the largest, most extravagant *falla* is ignited in the city's main square, Plaza Ayuntamiento, followed by a spectacular fireworks display called *Nit de Foc*, Night of Fire.

Before I left Madrid, everybody assured me that nobody reserves a room during *La Crema*, because everyone's out carousing. So I threw a few things into a small backpack, brought a minimal amount of cash—I heard slimy pickpockets liked to prey on roving revelers—and planned on staying up throughout the festivities.

The moment I stepped off my crowded bus and into the blazing sunshine of downtown Valencia, I knew I had entered a rambunctious realm. It was 1 p.m., and people of all ages were ambling around, chomping on street vendors' salty olives and roasted nuts, and sipping from bottles of beer or wine. Tired and thirsty, I bought a refreshing *horchata*, the milky, partially frozen Valencian drink made from *chufas* (earth almonds).

I strolled along, inspecting the enormous, grotesque *papier-mâché* statues of famous faces, such as Steven Spielberg, and silly scenes, such as a pudgy chef standing waist-deep in a huge pot of spaghetti. As I walked, I sensed the energy building around me. Then, a ground-trembling explosion shook me: Huge piles of fireworks burst into slate clouds of smoke and color not more than 15 feet away. I had stumbled upon *Las Mascletas*, a daily competition among neighborhoods for the loudest, most impressive display. For 10 minutes, everybody covered their ears, dogs barked wildly, and traffic froze. A bit rattled, but grinning irrepressibly, I expected an exhilarating demonstration for *Nit de Foc*.

I walked around for hours, marveling at the *fallas* and *ninots*, as well as the city's architecture, a mix of art nouveau and medieval. Crowds cheered for elaborately dressed men and women parading through the streets. I whistled and chanted, following the masses past the huge iron, glass and tile Mercado Central to a 17th-century church. There, people brought amazing floral arrangements to *La Virgen de los Desamparados*, the church's statue of The Virgin of the Forsaken, virtually covering her with thousands of flowers. I spent a lot of time taking in their aromas.

After the sun set and the men placed the fireworks inside the *fallas*, revelers throughout the city grew even more restless. Crowds of young people had been dancing obnoxiously in the streets for hours of unabashed debauchery, but the real party was about to begin. Just after midnight, *fallas* and *ninots* standing on various streets went up in flames, and I could feel the heat from 20 feet away. I made a game of running from street to street, guessing which star athlete or revered artist would be ignited next.

With the number of fires smoldering around me, I wasn't surprised to hear that, in 1851, the city's mayor outlawed the ritual. But the spirit of *Las Fallas* was irrepressible, and the ban didn't last.

In the main square, I jostled my way through hundreds of Spanish families, international tourists and local policemen to behold the largest *falla*, the vivid visage of Gulliver, hero of Jonathan Swift's scathing novel "Gulliver's Travels." He was several stories tall, staring at the crowd as if cursing such a grandiose display of frivolity. When the first round of firecrackers went off, the entire square erupted, whistling and yelling, jumping up and down with almost as much energy as the fireworks themselves. Showers of brilliantly hued sparks filled the sky from the *barrios*, echoing the blasts coming from the *falla*. Then, in a bittersweet bow, Gulliver sizzled into oblivion, releasing bright orange flares and plumes of smoke above the emptying square.

I worried that, after the final explosions, the celebrants would feel burned out. But no—this was Spain! As the fires fizzled, the heat of the people grew.

People feverishly spread throughout the city streets, billowing into local hot spots as though seeking a release.

On *Calle de Caballeros* in the *Barrio del Carmen*, a neighborhood stocked with cool bars and discos, I squeezed my way into a multi-story bar in a converted house, perfect for dancing. Soon, I realized my feet were throbbing more than the music. After nearly 20 hours awake, I had to sit down. All the plush couches were occupied by similarly exhausted young people, so I picked a corner on the floor near the bar entrance. I was nearly dozing off when a slim Spaniard spotted me, took my hand and said, "You can't be tired already!"

> **I was nearly dozing off when a slim Spaniard spotted me, took my hand and said, "You can't be tired already!"**

He promptly helped me up, introduced me to his two pals from Madrid, and invited me along to explore *la madrugada*—the dawn. My aching feet protested, but the rest of me wanted to continue celebrating. Spanish children ran wildly in the streets, leaving firecracker explosions in their wakes. We dodged them and ducked into a little bar decorated with posters of old actors and movies. As we sucked down drinks and listened to laid-back tunes, the guys told me this was their first *Fallas*, too. We compared impressions of the festival, and they toasted my bravery for traveling alone to it.

Then, curious about what happens after such an extravagant event, we went back out and walked around Valencia. It was a city asleep after a night of abandon. Despite warnings that thieves ruled the streets after *Las Fallas*, we glimpsed only workers determined to clean up. Amazingly, the place seemed spotless after just a few hours, and scant remnants of the night's decadence remained.

When we finally parted company, I boarded a packed bus headed to a reputedly quiet town with a serene beach. Sitting in the back of that bus after more than 24 hours of sensory overload, quiet was pretty much all I craved.

CARA NISSMAN *is a West Palm Beach, Florida-based writer who has contributed to Seventeen, Teen Vogue, Salon.com, The Palm Beach Post and The Boston Herald. Nissman, a past contributor to Europe From a Backpack, has traveled solo around Spain, Portugal, Ireland, France and Italy. She saves her pennies so she may explore more of the world.*

Barcelona
No Shoes, No Shirts, No Problems

jon azpiri

"Look at where we are!" Patrick shouted to me incredulously as we sat on a patio on *Las Ramblas* in Barcelona. It didn't matter to him that we were on the patio of McDonald's, the only restaurant we could afford, or that we were sipping on gazpacho that tasted like watered-down V8 juice. He just couldn't believe he was in Spain, away from his home in Sydney for the first time in his life. It wasn't the first time he had said this to me. He did it so often, he'd named his trip "Patrick's Look At Where We Are Tour 2000."

I had met Patrick on *Las Ramblas*, not long after I had arrived. He'd spotted me trudging along with my backpack and asked me if I needed a room. He had an extra bed at his place, and I'd failed to get in at the overly popular Kabul Hostel, so I quickly agreed.

Patrick was a burly, hard-drinking Australian who had taken a year off to travel the world. Once you got past his rough edges, however, you'd find a contagious, childlike optimism. Although he often missed the main tourist sites in a city, he would catch the smallest things. Children playing in a plaza, a brightly lit water fountain, the fact that you could buy a litre of wine at the grocery store for less than a dollar—these things filled Patrick with wonder. And he would inevitably exclaim, "Look at where we are!"

Patrick's open-minded approach to life often led us to new people. Men seemed to like him because he was always willing to buy a drink, and women were drawn to his rugged good looks and impish charm. Even though he couldn't speak a word of Spanish, he managed to beguile several local girls. I, on the other hand, was too reserved to chat up women, despite the fact that I was nearly fluent in Spanish, and even knew a few words of Catalan.

Over the next five days, a pattern emerged. Unlike Patrick, who seemed to revel in small moments, I insisted on seeing all the big sights. I would get up early and visit places like Parc Güell, La Sagrada Familia and the Picasso Museum, taking photos and writing in my journal, as if my trip were some sort of homework project, while Patrick spent the day sleeping off his hangover from the night before. Each night around 9, we would meet in our room, head out for dinner, then hit the town.

Our final night in "Barca," Patrick wanted to go out on a high note. We asked some locals what was the best nightclub in town, and they told us about La Terrazza, a giant monastery-turned-nightclub that was supposed to be the biggest party in Spain outside of Ibiza. Patrick's eyes lit up, and our plans were set. He invited some of the local girls he had met the night before. "This is going to be brilliant," he assured me.

We arrived at the club at ten o'clock, obscenely early by Spanish standards. Still, a line snaked its way around the entire *Poble Español*. I tried to persuade Patrick to go elsewhere, but he wouldn't hear of it. He wanted to experience the best nightclub in Barcelona.

Behind us in the endless queue was a group of Americans who were visiting Spain during their summer break from studying in England. They were wearing crisp dress shirts and freshly pressed khakis, and they shared Patrick's enthusiasm about the club. One of them, Derek, was studying economics, and the hour-plus we waited in line gave him plenty of time to explain the economic theories of John Maynard Keynes and John Kenneth Galbraith.

As we finally approached the front of the line, the doorman waved Patrick into the club. I followed as Patrick swaggered through the front door, but the squat, long-haired doorman stopped me.

"Excuse me, do you have an invitation?" he said.

"No. What invitation?" I replied.

"Tonight is invitation only. If you don't have one, you'll have to go."

"Wait a minute. You just let my friend in, and I know he doesn't have an invitation."

"Go away!" he said, shoving me aside.

As I scanned the rest of the crowd in line, it was pretty clear that I didn't get in because I didn't fit in. The club appealed to a techno/rave crowd, with women wearing mini-skirts, feathered boas and platform heels, and men wearing leather pants and spiked dog collars. Apparently, Patrick's shaggy hair, vintage cowboy shirt and motorcycle boots blended in with the crowd, and my V-neck sweater from The Gap didn't.

We were close to admitting defeat, but Scott was on a mission. "We're getting in there. I'll be back in fifteen minutes."

The smartly dressed Americans met the same hassle. They soon joined me on the street corner, sulking. We were close to admitting defeat, but Scott, Derek's friend from California, was on a mission. "We're getting in there. I'll be back in fifteen minutes."

While Scott scampered off, I considered leaving, but the Americans insisted that I wait. "Don't worry," Derek said. "Scott will get us in. I don't know how, but he'll get us in. He's gotten into a lot tougher places than this. He never fails."

I decided to stick around to see if Scott could work his magic. Ten minutes later, he came back with four tickets. He'd sweet-talked some local girls into giving him their V.I.P. passes. Since the girls had some friends who worked in the club, they knew they could get in anytime without them.

So we sauntered past the main lineup and, not five feet from where we had been rejected, walked in through the V.I.P. entrance. I took off my V-neck sweater; my plain gray T-shirt seemed to do the trick. Inside La Terrazza, crowds of Barcelona's most beautiful people bounced to the sound of bland techno music on a dance floor in an open courtyard. I finally found Patrick. He had been wondering where I was, while trying to score some Ecstasy.

Since I spoke Spanish, he wanted me to ask the locals where to find the Ecstasy. Apparently he thought it wasn't called "E", but "É" with one of those funny accents on it, and he needed my help. I was hesitant. I figured if I was ever going to be arrested, I didn't want it to be for translating a drug deal. Besides, I told him, the Spanish word for Ecstasy is "Ecstasy." It shouldn't be hard to explain.

Patrick scampered off, as did the Americans, and I found myself alone. A light rain sprinkled the dance floor. After the ordeal of getting into the club, the cool water on my face helped me relax. I began dancing, and I finally started to enjoy my last night in Barcelona.

As I danced, I would occasionally scan the area,

looking for Patrick. That's when I spotted the squat doorman who wouldn't let me in. Apparently he was on a break from watching the door, walking through the crowd with a girl on each of his tattooed arms. We locked eyes; he immediately lunged onto the dance floor and grabbed me.

But the doorman wasn't that big. I was at least 6 inches taller and outweighed him by 20 pounds. He started shoving me, and I didn't budge. This was all new to me. Back home in Canada, where doormen tended to be the size of mini-vans, I never got into fights with bouncers, let alone won one.

Two other doormen quickly jumped in to subdue me. One of them got me in a headlock and escorted me out of the club. As I stood outside on the sidewalk, where I had already spent much of the night, I rubbed my wrenched neck and realized that I'd just been a victim of Fashion Police brutality.

I pleaded with the other doormen to let me back in to find my friend, but they'd have none of it. The doormen were curious, however, about what I had done to get expelled. I told them I hadn't bothered anyone. Heck, I hadn't had a drink all night. "Well, there's your problem," joked one of the doormen. "You were probably the only sober guy in there."

The doormen continued chatting. At one point, a confused young British girl came out of the club and asked the doormen for help, and I stepped in to translate. From there, the conversation started to flow.

Before, I had needed Patrick to meet new people, but now I felt strangely liberated.

I started chatting with some of the other outcasts, people who had been thrown out because they were too drunk, or who were not allowed in because they weren't cool enough. There was a drunken Australian girl who was ejected but had to wait for her friend, because she didn't know how to get back to their hotel. There were two local guys who weren't allowed in even though their girlfriends were already in the club. They openly worried about all the guys in there hitting on their girlfriends, and I tried to comfort them by saying that the only guy approaching their girls was likely a burly Australian asking them for Ecstasy.

We club rejects spent the rest of the night telling stories, asking questions about each other and talking about where we were from. It was fun and interesting and, as a bonus, no one hassled me about my V-neck sweater from The Gap. Before I knew it, an hour or two had passed. I was enjoying myself more outside the club than I had inside it.

The sun was rising, and the club was closing up for the night. I finally reconnected with Patrick, who never managed to find any Ecstasy—or those local girls he had met the night before. "What happened to you?" he asked.

"I got thrown out."

"*You?*" he asked in a way that was almost insulting. "How is that possible?"

I told him about my altercation with the doorman. Patrick went into a rage. "Let's get 'em," he said, heading back into the club to look for the doorman. I had known Patrick all of five days, and here he was willing to beat the hell out of a total stranger on my behalf. I grabbed him and told him it wasn't worth it.

"But he ruined your last night in Barcelona," he said.

"No, he didn't," I replied. We were standing on a nondescript corner outside the club, and I was thinking of the outcast friends I had met that night. "Look at where we are!"

JON AZPIRI *is a writer and editor based in Vancouver, Canada. Being of Basque heritage, his favorite part of Spain, by far, is the Basque Country, where no one judges him on his penchant for V-neck sweaters.*

> Like all great travelers, I have seen more than I remember, and remember more than I have seen.
> — Benjamin Disraeli

Madrid

Madrid
Close Quarters
lauren guza

two months into my study-abroad program in England, I was convinced of my own invincibility. After all, I'd ridden the London subway without getting caught in the automatic doors more than twice. I'd trained myself to look to the *right* first when crossing the street. And I'd learned to speak British with admirable fluency.

When the university announced we would be given a week free from classes to focus on preparing for exams, I promptly booked a train ticket to Spain. I set out for Waterloo Station muttering flimsy justifications about the value of life experience. Dawn hadn't yet seeped through the gray stillness, and the coming day was deep and wide and inviting. I scoffed at the airplanes taking off from Heathrow, cutting the sky with their hard upward angles. How blind those people are, I thought. Think of what they miss from 30,000 feet.

The first leg of the trip, from London to Paris, involved an anticlimactic passage under the English Channel. The conductor warned us that soon we would all be descending into the darkest depths of oceanic transportation, and anybody who suffered from claustrophobia, back pain, pregnancy or a really painful paper cut should please alert an attendant if requiring assistance. After this deliciously ominous introduction to the Chunnel, it was a bit disappointing when the 20-minute ride revealed itself to be not unlike a Los Angeles freeway tunnel at midnight.

I'd been ridiculously conservative in allowing myself most of the day to get to my connecting train, so I ended up spending six hours huddled beside my suitcase in the alarmingly cold Paris station, forced to keep warm by eating gooey chocolate pastries. I had christened the suitcase "Croque" (pronounced "Craaaawk," with an obnoxious American accent), in honor of the perfectly melted *croque-monsieur* sandwich I'd eaten at a sidewalk café—and because I had to call him *something* when I spoke to him.

Despite its allure, Paris was merely a word printed on my itinerary, a logistical connection necessary for reaching my ultimate destination: Madrid. A red-gold name that made me think of spiced afternoons and Hemingway stories and orange peels. When the electronic board finally informed me that my train would leave in five minutes from Platform 7, I dragged lazy Croque toward the tracks, and within seconds was spectacularly lost, trying to communicate my situation to a nearby employee. My knowledge of French is derived almost entirely from Pepé Le Pew cartoons, and this particular fellow seemed to think my frantic inarticulateness was quite comedic. When I finally wrestled directions out of him, sprinted to my platform and leaped wildly through the train doors, I had only a moment to revel in oxygen-depleted glory before the engine began to nudge us out of the station.

Staggering down the narrow hallway, I located the door of the cabin that would be mine for the overnight trip to Madrid. I threw it open, peered inside and realized quite suddenly that when I'd called to book a bedroom, they'd thought I said closet. I, though perfectly accustomed to college dorm rooms and childhood games of sardine, could not believe that a space so small was meant to contain human life. It was about eight feet wide, and two pairs of chairs, metal with cracked polyester cushions, faced each other in such a way that any two people sitting in them would rub knees. The walls were plastic painted to look like wood, and trimmed with grooves that suggested four fold-out beds might actually emerge into this mouse hole. A single sink, sterile and separate, seemed to smirk at me from the corner. The windows were shrouded in stiff, institutional curtains. The closet's purple shadows were barely dissipated by its one naked light bulb.

And suffocating the cabin with her wide, full body and expressionless face was The Woman—and her smell. It was a thick, fleshy odor, a scent of sweat petrified in crevices of skin. My breath caught in me, and I resisted the urge to run, thinking that might be rude. She'd nodded in my direction when I first opened the door, but now seemed barely to notice me as I wedged Croque into a corner. We were sharing space, sharing air, sharing lives, and yet her eyes wouldn't meet mine. It occurred to me that perhaps she didn't speak English, but even my nervous Spanish and barely existent French seemed only to confuse her, so we resorted to a vague vocabulary of grunts and shy smiles. She busied herself with her baby, whom I hadn't noticed at first, but who now gurgled and bubbled at me through rolls of skin and saliva.

Though it was still early, I dove onto the top bunk the moment the attendant flipped it down from the wall. After contributing to the heavenly aroma in the cabin by changing her young son's diaper, my roommate turned out the light, and we lay there, about two feet from each other, yet so very separate. I watched the smudge of moonlight through the tiny window for hours as the train lurched across the land. I thought how strange the shadows looked, how even the lumps my feet made in the thin blanket seemed unfamiliar and disconnected.

I kept my sweatshirt tucked close around my nose to ward off the smell, preferring death by suffocation to toxic inhalation. As sleep began to play with my eyelids, I had the hazy sensation that the walls were converging, mummifying my body in glass and plastic shadows.

The banging on the door sounded distant at first, like a nearly forgotten dream, but when it persisted I half-consciously opened my eyes and stared into the darkness. It must have been 3 or 4 in the morning, and I'd only just fallen asleep. I groaned and tried to ignore the pounding, but after several rounds of it my roommate rose, unhooked the latch and let the greenish light flood our room. I barely registered the low, hurried voice of the train attendant, her stilted English muffled by the night, but I jolted up from the mattress when I heard her whisper to my roommate: "Excuse me please, but the police. They want to speak to you. They need for you to come. Yes, please can you go outside now?"

> "Excuse me please, but the police. They want to speak to you."

Of course, I thought. Of course the foreign police want to interrogate my roommate in the middle of the night, in a land I don't recognize, in this tiny room where nobody knows my name or my story. I could hear the heavy coats and tense murmuring of the officers shuffling in the hallway. For several minutes, the attendant wove fragmented English and clumsy French into her native Spanish, a language I'd known the day before, but which now seemed distant and impenetrable. Recognizing the confusion in my roommate's eyes, I leaned toward the door and tried to translate the English into French for her. After one or two fumbled words, I remembered I didn't speak French and sheepishly retreated to my mattress to hide.

And yet, without further conversation, they left her. Never mind, they said. We're sorry. While I was relieved to see them go, it was rather alarming to find myself locked into this space with a possible fugitive from the law and only Croque to protect me. Sleep did not come for a long time. The train axles moaned wearily and the darkness felt wet and cold on my skin. Yet the air seemed fresh and tinged with adventure. I thought about what it means to be alone, and what it means to be alive, and I felt the two were joined somehow, in the world of this room, in the smells and the breathing and the purple air.

In the morning, Spain came bounding through the window in streaming, giddy strides. My first view of it was the sunrise—turquoise sky and orange hills, and the spray of foamy light on the cabin walls. The train whistle made musical punctuation. I touched the crisp page in my passport where the blank space had been surprised by an inky-red Madrid stamp. My eyes itched from the sleepless hours, but I woke Croque and folded my bed back into the wall neatly, watching my roommate bundle her son into her arms and disappear into the Spanish morning.

The room was suddenly quite empty, yet it seemed friendly, like it knew me somehow. As Croque and I moved slowly into the crowds and colors and voices, we let ourselves be swept up, feeling very much alive.

LAUREN GUZA *graduated from Middlebury College in 2005, with a degree in English/creative writing. Her travel-writing career began when she was about 3. She would follow her imaginary friends around the back yard, making up stories about their adventures. Lauren teaches high-school English in Los Angeles, as a member of Teach for America. She plans to spend the next few years teaching, writing and wandering the world—with both real and imaginary friends.*

Madrid

Life as a Metro Musician

garrick aden-buie

my voice echoes down the tunnel that connects lines 2 and 10 of Metro de Madrid, filling up the space left empty by the stale air and white-tiled walls. Fifty meters above me, it's a January afternoon in Spain, cold and clear.

Down here, I'm singing classic American rock songs and playing guitar in the subway. My stage is the longest passageway in the entire metro network, without the typical moving sidewalks that would drown out my acoustic guitar and ruin my chances of eating the supper I'm singing for.

A short, elderly woman, wearing an oversized mink

...at swishes lazily against her hips, drops a coin in the guitar case at my feet. A group of rowdy boys walks by behind her and starts singing in mumbled approximations of English words. I dance with them for a moment, not caring if they throw some coins my way. After all, I'm a metro musician in Madrid, and I am living a dream.

I've always had a peculiar fascination with the concept of imposing music on a disinterested, passive crowd. When I visited New York City, I spent nearly an entire day in Times Square listening to a Boyz II Men wanna-be band belt out gospel standards in four-part harmonies. Years later, I went to Montreal and ended up following around a street performer who banged away on a cheap acoustic guitar in minus-10-degree weather, singing pop tunes for drunken college students. Neither was that good. It was the idea of playing to the unknown faces of the casual passersby that attracted me.

Now it's my junior year abroad in Madrid, and I've discovered metro musicians: Eastern Europeans slinging accordions and car-hopping metro trains; gypsy vocalists singing off-key *a capella* through karaoke amplifiers; a German opera singer wailing in dissonant harmonies that can be heard over metro rumblings two cars away. My dream, once an idle fascination, is staring me in the face. Every station I walk through, every street corner in the center of Madrid, every empty bench in every park looks to me like a potential stage. Spaces like these simply don't exist in my hometown in Pennsylvania.

Finally, I set a day, pick an hour, find a spot and change my guitar strings. This will be my debut. I strap on my guitar bag and set out for the metro, determined to live this dream. I get out at Plaza de España and climb the set of escalators that lead to the long connecting hallway. I set myself up in the midpoint of the tunnel, break out my guitar and kick my gig bag out into an aesthetically pleasing position at my feet. I strike an open chord and the walls glare at me, indignantly white. Ignoring them, I launch into Mick Jagger's *Sympathy for the Devil* as the first wave of passengers turns the corner and crosses my stage.

The public comes and goes in tides: businessmen with confident strides and pink silk neckties; Latin-American immigrants with ambling demeanors; elderly *madrileños* with their relaxed paces and smoothly worn features; university students in bold colors half-running to make their connections.

Responses are varied. Some pluck change from their pockets or purses as if their recent New Year's resolutions read, *Give money to subway musicians*. Others nod their heads, alter their step or take off their headphones. Some do everything they can not to make eye contact, but still smile at the dancing American playing guitar when he finally catches their eye. Others slow down and take their time walking by, then later retrace their steps to toss some coins at my feet. They tell me they're sorry; it's all the loose change they have. I smile and sing even louder.

Two hours later, I find myself under the vast Madrid sky again. The sun is off in the corner, bathing buildings in a crimson glow. I pause to contemplate the magnificent *Palacio Real* at sundown on the other side of the *Rio Manzanares*, and I jingle the 6.37 euros in small coins that fill my pocket.

I've found a secret in this city, I realize. Each day is a dream—sometimes a dream I've had for years and others a dream that I invent as I go, but they're all worthy of pursuit. These are not the dreams that simply come to me when I close my eyes. They are more profound, more real; they require my active participation. I'm living in the moment, and in this moment I find myself walking down the street that leads me to home.

GARRICK ADEN-BUIE *spent 365 days in Spain, where, in addition to the occasional afternoon playing guitar in the metro, he taught English to 12-year-olds and volunteered at a center for the homeless. His adventures led him to travel through all but two of the autonomous regions of Spain, but his heart will forever be in Madrid. Home is a relative term for Garrick, but his strongest ties are in Chicago.*

Madrid
Mugged!
pamela barrus

There was no mistaking what was about to happen: the running footsteps, the flash of a red T-shirt, the glimpse of desperation. Instinctively, I bent over, clutching my purse to my chest. Two hands intruded on my body, trying to grab my purse. *You're gonna have to fight me for it*, I muttered to myself through clenched teeth. Time slowed. Strange how the finest detail can etch itself in one's memory, yet I don't know how I ended up rolling around in the middle of the street, fighting an attacker.

It was the end of August, and I had been living in Madrid with a local family, studying Spanish. The legendary summer heat drove *madrileños* out of their houses and into the street all night, every night—and I joined them, certainly a better alternative than sleeping naked under a wet towel in a hot room, splashing myself periodically with water from a glass next to the bed.

This was just another suffocating hot night. I was on my way to dinner with my proper English friend, Ruth, who also was in Madrid studying Spanish. Her sister Fiona and their mother, Joy, who had flown down from London for the weekend, accompanied us.

As we stepped out from their hotel onto the crowded street, I looked at Fiona's platform shoes, mini-skirt and very blonde hair, and thought: *You look like a victim.* Joy dangled a purse off her arm. Spain, and especially Madrid, had a reputation for brazen muggers, but generally they attacked confused-looking tourists who wore running shoes, baseball caps and shorts.

I could pass as Spanish, so I felt immune. I was merely going to dinner as I had a hundred times before. It was 10:30 at night, early by Madrid standards, and the streets were full of people. The next moment, I was flat on the ground, rolling around in the middle of Calle Atocha.

He's got both hands on the purse, which means he doesn't have a knife, I breathed with some relief. In

> **I looked at Fiona's platform shoes, mini-skirt and very blonde hair, and thought:** *You look like a victim.*

the middle of a real drama, it's amazing one can think so clearly. *Too bad I don't have a free hand to poke his eyes out.* My attacker and I made small grunts at each other. *Don't break the skin! Don't break the skin!* I warned myself as I tried to bite his arm. *This guy could be a drug addict and I'll catch some fatal disease.* Somewhere, in what seemed another dimension, I could hear a chorus of women screaming nonsensically.

What's going on around me? I had no way of knowing. All I could see, all I could focus on, was the mugger's arm, taut with determination, trying to snatch my purse away. I knew I couldn't waste the slightest bit of energy to look up at him. If I did, I would lose, which was out of the question.

Suddenly, it was over. Someone helped me off the ground. A hundred people, it seemed, were gaping at me. I glanced toward the sidewalk and saw a thin, ratty-looking man in a red T-shirt, his shoulders held back by another man.

"*Qué te jodas! Puta madre!*" I yelled as I stepped toward him, ready to deliver a good kick in the nuts. One can become fluent in any language when the occasion arises. "Don't go near him," a voice to the side warned in accented English. I stopped and looked around. The voice was right. I had no idea what had gone on around me, and perhaps the situation was still dangerous. I had my purse, and as much as I wanted to give the final kick to my mugger, he could make another grab for me. There was no way I was going through that again.

Everyone in the street stood about, not quite knowing what to do. My attacker shook himself free from the man who was trying to hold him and shot off down the street like a jackrabbit. The crowd closed in around me. I heard the word *Moro* several times. For months, the Spanish newspapers had blamed a skyrocketing increase in assaults on illegal immigrants from North Africa who were pouring into Spain.

The vision in my right eye was blurring. I turned to my friend Ruth. "Does this eye look OK to you?"

"Pamela, you look like you've got a bit of a knock there."

My head was reeling. I looked down at my once-blue dress, now a shade of unspeakable filth. Ruth's mother was wiping blood from her leg with a tissue; Fiona was standing on the sidewalk crying.

"Joy, are you OK? That's a nasty scrape on your leg. And Fiona, what happened to you?"

"Mother slipped while she was trying to help you beat off that guy, and Fiona is distraught because she's been attacked twice this year," Ruth explained.

"Well, I could really use a drink right now. I think I need to drink *a lot*," I said, examining my wounds. We took a taxi to the Plaza Mayor, not only the heart of glorious old Madrid, but one of Spain's most striking arcaded plazas. They propped me in a chair at an outdoor restaurant and ordered a bottle of my favorite red wine. It was past midnight now, and the sweltering air still hung heavy. Despite the overpriced restaurants that lined the perimeter, the plaza was filled with hundreds of people escaping their hot apartments.

We spent the next few hours trying to piece together the evening's events.

"Pamela, I think your attacker rushed up beside you and slammed you in the face with his elbow," Ruth's mother theorized. "I tried to help you but wasn't very successful, I'm afraid."

"Well, I was looking for something to hit him with, and all I had was the *Time Out* guide to Madrid. So, I hit him over the head with that. Not very effective, actually," Ruth said. "Did you know a man came up, who I thought was going to help, and he ripped my purse off me and ran? I think he had a knife."

Fiona offered her opinion: "I saw something metal in his hand, Ruthie. He had a knife. I'm sure of it."

"What happened next? I was in mortal combat with this guy. I had no idea what was going on around me. All I could hear was screaming."

"Two men came to the rescue. One ran after the second thief and got my purse back with everything in it; the second man got the attacker off you."

Well, statistics had finally caught up with me. Here I was, the great professional vagabond. I had blithely traveled alone all over the world. Fiona was the one who looked like a target. And now a common street mugger had jumped me in Madrid, a city I called my second home. I pressed the ice-filled towel against my injured eye. How vulnerable we can be!

A few days later, during our Spanish class, Ruth pointed out, "You know, I don't think we properly thanked those two men who helped us. Do you think if we wrote a letter to the newspaper, they would somehow see it?"

In the most melodramatic style I could muster in Spanish, I recounted the story of two brave Spanish men who came to the rescue of four women, their heroic actions preventing a tragic outcome. We wanted to thank profusely these two men for their initiative. We signed our letter Pamela Barrus, Laguna Beach, California, USA, and Ruth Biziou, Bristol, England, and e-mailed it to the national newspaper, *El País*.

Three days later, muscles I didn't even know I had shrieked in pain; I felt like a truck had run over me. Ruth came by to visit, waving the newspaper. "*Agradecimiento a dos valientes* ... Pamela, they printed it!" I jumped out of bed and looked at the paper. *El País* had indeed printed it—not among the "Letters to the Editor," but in the "Opinion" section. We were famous.

Aches and pains now vanished, Ruth and I hurried over to the restaurant on the Plaza Mayor to show the letter to the waiter who had given me the iced towels. Filled with pride, he bowed and asked our permission to borrow the newspaper for a moment. Waiters from every restaurant on the plaza passed by every few minutes, filling our wine glasses. Plates of *tapas* were placed in front of us.

"Ruth, we must be the first people in the history of the Plaza Mayor to ever get anything free."

"Well, I think it's bravo to us."

"You know," I said, "I think this black eye was worth it."

A VAGABOND *since birth, Pamela Barrus has idled her time away traveling solo in nearly 200 countries, enjoying the glorious freedom of public buses, cargo ships and trains. She has authored two guidebooks on castle hotels in Europe and a third on San Diego, California, as well as articles for national magazines. Tutoring and local tour-guiding help pay for her habit.*

Madrid

Her

dave munsell

I'd been warned: Never go to Puerta del Sol in Madrid. The study-abroad people had said, "You've heard about the Bermuda Triangle, right? Well, Sol is the Madrid Triangle. All of your possessions just seem to disappear." They'd even gone so far as to map out the no-go area for us. But sometimes, I can be a punk-ass kid.

With my wallet in my front pocket and a clear head, I step out of the metro and into Puerta del Sol. Honestly, the Bermuda Triangle could not possibly hold this much culture. Sol is a place you just have to see. It is the Times Square, Las Ramblas, Les Champs-Élysées of Madrid. The drinks are pricier, the people are louder, and the place is jammed full of people and cars. Neon and blinking lights add to the visual excitement, and a 50-foot-tall neon Tío Pepe watches over his plaza from high above the buildings.

I start walking. To my left, a band plays South American tunes loudly, attracting a lively melange of locals and tourists. Streetcars whiz by, weaving among pedestrians and each other, carrying the patrons of the night to their destinations. Jazz is on my mind tonight, and I head for Café Populart.

The smoky bar and cool music flood my senses. I can hear it, see it, smell it in the air; I can taste it. I breathe it in. The walls are covered with pictures of the greats—Miles, Coltrane, Brubeck. I see retired instruments, and fliers for both past and upcoming events. This place is clutch and I am in gear.

I am one Cuba Libre down when I see Her, halfway across the smoke-filled bar. At first glance, she looks like just another middle-aged woman who has seen years of life, good and bad. She does not interest me.

Then she begins to dance. I watch her through the haze. She moves to the beat and lives the groove, allowing the flow to penetrate her every pore and nerve. I venture inside my head, attempting to get inside hers. She knows she is aging, but why let that stop her? Those hips can still carve curves in the smoky air. She sees herself in a red Spanish dress, with ruffles that flood to the ground and bells that tinkle with every movement. She's wearing her favorite dancing shoes, broken in from countless nights on this floor. Young again and without a care, she sees herself as perfect as ever.

I am staring. She catches the beat of the bass. The musician's fingers meander over the strings and she sways, dips, stomps her feet to his tune. She remembers a club that is not much different from this one, way back from her youth. Only the music is the same. Deep in her imagination, she has returned to that club. Familiar as ever, the faces surrounding her smile as she takes center stage. She has the spotlight. The dance floor clears and the light strikes her every movement, accentuating her youthful beauty. Continuing to move, graceful, yet forceful, she is empowered. She knows everyone is watching, but she dances as if no one is.

She knows everyone is watching, but she dances as if no one is.

The night grows late, and the jazz musicians puff their last cigarettes and finish their cocktails onstage. I can feel their music coming to an end, and she can, too. She shakes those hips, then cuts them sharp in one final twist, and her night of dancing is over. Sitting back in her chair with an overwhelming sense of enjoyment, her eyes are beautiful and beaming.

As she takes her pack of Ducados out of her little Spanish purse, she waits a moment to light one up and glances around the room. She catches my eye. With a little smile, I wink, and she knows I've been watching her dance. She turns back toward the stage and I can see the flicker of her lighter. Inhaling deeply, she smokes her cigarette with great satisfaction. She has earned this moment. The cloud of smoke crosses the threshold of her lips and rises into the air, lingering for a moment before mixing into the haze.

DAVE MUNSELL *is a fourth-year student at Syracuse University, studying political science. He spent a semester in Madrid and was able to explore many cultures throughout Europe. He hopes to join the U.S. State Department's Foreign Service so he can work and travel abroad.*

Madrid

First, un Bocata de Calamares

kip wilson

"I'm starving." I rubbed my stomach, blinking at my Spanish boyfriend to see what he would do about it. We were waiting for the Pink #8 subway train that would take us from the airport to Madrid.

Bernardo smiled. "We'll go have a sandwich when we get downtown."

"At el Diamante? The bar with the *bocata de calamares*?"

"*Sí.*" Bernardo nodded.

"Ooooh." I pictured the place in my mind: waiters in white shirts and black vests, carrying trays while constantly scurrying between the bar and tables.

Bernardo had taken me there on my first trip to Spain. I remembered how we'd stood at the bar because it was cheaper. Maybe we'd sit down this time as a welcome-to-Spain luxury. I felt excited.

While we waited, I grabbed the 10-ride ticket we had just bought and stashed it away between my wallet and my passport, safe in my purse, then secured that in my backpack. I'd rearrange everything once we got to the hotel. I bounced up and down on the balls of my feet as the train finally pulled in. The train was about half-full, but as we got closer to El Kilómetro Cero (kilometer zero) at the city center, more and more people crowded into our car.

We made it over to the Light Blue #1 train and were on our way. I leaned my head forward onto Bernardo's shoulder. He wrapped an arm around me and held us both up, his other hand gripping one of the central poles. As we pulled into the Sol station, people packed into the car all around us, wedging themselves behind us, beside us, and finally between us.

I took a step back to avoid the stale breath of the sweaty stranger who pressed his floppy beer belly around the central pole and into my hip. Bernardo now stood two people away, staring into space above the passengers' heads. Sweaty beer-belly man whipped out a handkerchief to clear away the beads of moisture that had gathered on his forehead. I could escape by only a few millimeters. This was becoming the longest subway ride of my life.

Finally, we pulled into the next station. Once the train emptied out and Bernardo stepped in close to me again, I breathed a sigh of relief. The next stop was ours: Atocha. We were almost at el Diamante!

"Hey, your backpack's open." Bernardo reached over to pull my pack's top strap, which was flopping over my shoulder.

"Huh?" I frowned. I knew I had buckled it tightly back at the airport. It must've come undone somehow. But as I pulled the pack around to the front of me and began digging through my books and papers, my stomach lurched. I had totally screwed up, and it was too late to do anything about it.

"Damn—it's gone!" My purse, which I had so carefully tucked inside my backpack, had vanished. My passport, travel money, credit cards, wallet, and even the keys to my Scion back home—they were all gone. I couldn't believe it. My heart pounded in my chest. Things like that didn't happen to me. Only a total travel rookie would make that kind of mistake.

Then I remembered. "Beer-belly man!" I rolled my eyes.

"¿Qué?" Bernardo frowned.

"Just this creepy guy. Ugh! He must've been working with a partner." I pictured someone sneaking into my pack while he distracted me. "Damn, damn, damn. What should I do?" I pushed a strand of hair back behind my ear.

"First of all," Bernardo paused, calm and strong, "we should get *un bocata de calamares y una caña.*" He pointed out the window, where I could see the sign for our stop, Atocha.

I sucked in a breath. "Huh?" How could he think of a sandwich at a time like this? My stuff was gone! How could he think of anything else? And a sandwich? A sandwich. A mouthwatering sandwich of crispy calamari on crusty bread, slathered with garlicky mayonnaise. With a refreshing beer on the side.

I couldn't help smiling. Maybe everything would be OK. So I had no identification or money. So what? I shrugged my shoulders. It was liberating. I had nothing else to steal. And I was in Spain. I smiled as I shouldered my backpack and followed Bernardo out of the train.

I was about to eat the best calamari sandwich I had ever tasted.

KIP WILSON *is a writer from Boston, Massachusetts, with a Ph.D. in German from S.U.N.Y. Albany. She is a regular backpacker-around-Europe and was never robbed during her travels, until the summer of 2005.*

Madrid
Off the Map
evan l. balkan

I'm standing at the intersection of Guzman el Bueno and Ferdinand de los Rios in Madrid. I'm staring up at two apartment buildings, unsure which is the one that holds great significance for me, and which means nothing to me at all. Neither one is particularly alluring; between them hang power lines where three little birds have taken up temporary residence. On the ground floor, a man in a business suit enters a shop called Paulo. Across the street, Casa de Cataluna is covered in red graffiti.

I've walked the better part of four hours to get to this block, so far from the *pension* where I'm staying that I've just walked off the little folded map I'm using.

It feels like a thousand miles from the Prado or the Plaza Mayor. In fact, the most interesting thing I've seen along the way here is a 7-Eleven convenience store. I hadn't realized one could find them outside of the United States. Eschewing Twinkies and Ring-Dings, I have made my interminably plodding way toward the apartment buildings at Guzman el Bueno and Ferdinand de los Rios.

I've stared up at some interesting apartment blocks over the years. The shabby tenement in Brooklyn where my immigrant grandparents raised my mother and two aunts. The utterly cheerless concrete slab in Nuuk, Greenland, that houses a full 1% of the country's population. The low-slung, three-story building built into a hill in Neuchatel, Switzerland, where I watched my cousin slowly die from a lung infection. My own Georgian/Federal conglomeration where I live in Baltimore, across from the ellipse at Johns Hopkins—the same place F. Scott Fitzgerald looked upon when he wrote "Afternoon of an Author."

Now, here I am in Madrid, a recent college graduate, four months into a backpacking trip across Europe with my buddy Woody. Woody is a great friend, that rare type that I could stand to be with 24 hours a day for four and a half months. We'd seen some fascinating things since landing in London last August. We trekked and railed across the U.K., ferried over to France, traveled through Belgium, Holland, Germany, Switzerland, Italy, Austria and Slovenia, then arced along the Mediterranean back into Italy, Monaco, France and, finally, Spain. In Barcelona, we were still the best of friends. By Madrid, we were the best of friends and we needed a break from each other.

So we agreed to split up every morning after breakfast and meet again at night to spend our last *pesetas* in search of cheap beer and young women. It was my suggestion to split up, but according to our respective linguistic skills, I navigated the French-speaking locales, and Woody was in charge of Italy and Spain. Now, I had to figure out directions, museum admissions and meals with my limited grasp of Spanish, which roughly incorporated the following: "*Dos huevos, por favor*" (Two eggs, please), "*Mira a los zapatos verde*" (Look at the green shoes), and "*Budweiser, la cerveza official de la Copa Mundial*" (Budweiser, the official beer of the World Cup).

I was heading way across town from our *pension* to find the place where my father had lived some 30 years earlier.

But grating on each other's nerves aside, I wanted to be alone on this day. I was heading way across town from our *pension* to find the place where my father had lived some 30 years earlier. That place was the corner of Guzman el Bueno and Ferdinand de los Rios.

My father is not Spanish. Like my mother, he grew up in Brooklyn. But my father's family had financial resources. As soon as my father's brother was old enough, he left the United States and became, for all intents and purposes, a European. In the 20-plus years that he lived in Europe, Uncle Lew came back to the United States only once. Despite seeing "Blazing Saddles," he didn't feel compelled to stay. He was living in Spain when my father crossed the Atlantic and joined him.

Eventually, my father settled into one of the apartment buildings across from where I'm now standing. As I stare up at them, I think perhaps even he wouldn't be able to tell which he lived in; for all I know, things have changed drastically. But I'd rather assume that the place looks precisely the way it did when my father lived there, remaining suspended in time, in the unreal years that came before me.

So I stand and I stare, eventually drawing a small crowd of people who stare also, looking for the thing I've fixated upon: a jumper? A fire? A damsel in distress? Even if I spoke Spanish, even if I could get across what I'm feeling, even if I had the words in English to explain the ethereal nature of all existence, I would be speechless.

Eventually, the people looking skyward disperse, satisfied that I'm staring at something they can't see, or something they have no interest in. Of course, it's both these things. And when I get my fill, I, too, walk away. I think about the wild nature of events, trying to imagine a day when a child of mine—one I can scarcely imagine, born by a woman I do not yet know—will stand some place more than 3,000 miles from home, over an ocean, in another country and culture, and marvel at an otherwise nondescript intersection on the outskirts of Madrid, in the way I just have.

EVAN L. BALKAN *teaches writing and literature at the Community College of Baltimore County in Maryland. His fiction and nonfiction, mostly in the areas of travel and outdoor recreation, have appeared in many publications throughout the United States, as well as Canada, England, Australia and Romania. He is the author of "60 Hikes Within 60 Miles: Baltimore." He lives in Lutherville, Maryland, with his wife, Shelly, and daughters, Amelia and Molly.*

Madrid
Robbed in the Rastro

salina ronderos

I tightened my purse strap before entering the scene: a mob of consumers and vendors negotiating over merchandise under hundreds of colorful canopies spanning several blocks in downtown Madrid. The capital city's celebrated flea market, known as El Rastro, is held every Sunday in the Plaza de Cascorro. It's the best place to find deals on last-minute souvenirs, but it's also one of the best places—No. 2 behind the subway—for thieves to prey on unsuspecting tourists.

I'd been warned about the Rastro, but the temptation of shopping for memorabilia in this vibrant marketplace was too great. I figured that keeping my purse snug under my armpit was good enough.

I mean, I'd been in Spain for two months now. I had traveled west to Salamanca and recounted the tales of Lazarillo de Tormes; east to Valencia, where I danced in the streets with hundreds honoring San José; north to the plains of Léon to see Europe's most celebrated and glorious 13th-century stained glass; and south to Sevilla, where I had been overcome by the power and beauty of flamenco dancers in the city's central courtyard. I was practically a citizen of Spain, right? And it was Easter Sunday, the holiest of days in Catholicism. Nothing bad would happen.

My cousin had joined me in Spain that week, and before his flight home, we decided to buy souvenirs from this country we had come to adore. Not 12 steps into the market, a piece of merchandise I could not pass up caught my eye. Two men were printing an eclectic mix of surnames on bullfighting posters. Colorful and bold, these posters featured the idolized matador dancing with his worthy opponent in the ring. They announced the time and location of the next fight, with the names of the matadors who were to show their mastery that day. Three names usually appear, and each matador typically challenges two bulls, one at a time. If you saw the names "Joselito" and "El Chulo," you were in for a real treat.

I had become fascinated with bullfights, and now this poster man was making it possible for my name to be printed among these legendary and suave *hombres*. I knew it was a cheesy Hollywood gimmick, but I couldn't resist! I was not alone. Dozens of Americans and Brits crowded the area in anticipation of being the next faux-fighter in print. I contemplated a crafty name to print on my poster. RONDEROS, I finally decided.

Then I looked under my left arm, where I held my purse ever so close, and my wallet was gone. Fright and despair drowned my excitement over the poster. The blood from my head shot straight to my stomach, taking all my oxygen with it. Lightheaded and breathless, I turned to my cousin and said, "I've just been robbed." It happened so quickly, I didn't feel a thing.

All was silent. My ears fell deaf to the hundreds of people making deals all around me, and my body grew numb. Then, an angel appeared.

Now, my friend Nancy taught me to believe in guardian angels, but I didn't know they provided transatlantic service, and I always thought that mine would be delicate, resembling my matriarchal ancestors, perhaps. This angel tapped my shoulder.

Carefully, slowly, I turned around to face a vagrant wearing a tattered maroon shirt. Nappy, fire-engine-red dreds were twisted upon his head, and silver- and gold-capped teeth filled his mouth. Without speaking, he said with a point of his finger, "It was her. She stole your wallet." He kept walking; his job here was done. I turned to confront my enemy, just as carefully.

She was a young girl with long, dark hair, standing

in front of me with two friends. Some Americans I met traveling through Segovia had just told me that an increasing number of young South American girls were robbing tourists and locals alike on the subway and in the outdoor markets. The girls, who couldn't have been older than 17, stood there watching the poster man.

With slight hesitation, I got the attention of the girl standing in the middle: "*¿Tu tienes mi bolsa?*" I forgot that the word for wallet in Spanish is *carrera*, but "purse" would work just the same.

"*No*," she answered, with innocent eyes.

Her cohorts began searching the ground around us as if they were doing me a favor. The girl to my right exclaimed in broken English, "Oh my Gaah," as if she were sympathetic to my situation. The girl in the middle, who appeared to be the leader of the pack, motioned as if she was going to open her purse for my perusal, but I stopped her. Was my American conscience preventing me from accusing her—innocent until proven guilty? I let her walk away.

Quickly, I reconsidered: I could stand here and do nothing, and still not have my wallet, or I could follow the girls and try to retrieve the property that I only *thought* they had. I decided I would not go gentle into that good fight: I raged!

Darting through the canopies, passing merchants and pushing people out of my path, I followed the alleged thieves through the Rastro. All five feet of me bobbed and weaved through the streets of Madrid. I knew I had to keep my distance, but my vertically challenged stature prevented me from trailing too far behind. My inner monologue began moving as fast as my feet: "What are you doing?" Fear said. "You're in a foreign country, running frantically through an enormous market. There are three of them and one of you, and you don't even know if your cousin is behind you." Denial interrupted: "Wait a second. This isn't happening to you. Check your purse one more time." Determination stepped in. "Hey, they stole something that belongs to you, and you have every right to reclaim it." Finally, My Rights shouted, "Move your rear and get your purse, because if you don't, you are screwed!"

I closed in on the girls within half a block. They walked together in perfect sync, arms linked, tilting their conniving heads to see what the middle girl was holding. I knew they were surveying the spoils—I knew they were searching through my wallet. Without hesitation, and without evidence, I grabbed hold of the middle girl's baby-blue jacket and turned her around to face me. Lo and behold, in her grimy hands was my innocent little wallet.

We were all shocked. I was shocked that it was true, and they were shocked that they got caught. With the foulest feelings of anger and personal attack, I cursed at the girl to her face. Now, I don't know how much English the girl knew, but next to love, I think cussing someone out is understood universally. I snatched my wallet from her with my right hand, her jacket still in my left. I released her with a forceful shove, then grabbed her again while I inspected my wallet to make sure nothing was missing. Nothing was. Fortunately for me, her comrades stood paralyzed, defeated.

My cousin had been behind me all the way. I walked away with 60 Euro, my International Student ID Card, one debit card—basically all the money I had left—and my dignity. Next time, though, I think I'll just be more careful in a known high-theft locale.

NOT QUITE AS EXCITING *as her days spent climbing Il Duomo in Florence, or eating tapas near the mysterious Dragon Tree in the Canary Islands, Salina Ronderos is currently a freelance writer in southern California. She is always looking for a way to get back to Europe.*

Pamplona
& the Camino

Madrid
Animal Instincts
lawrence schimel

I don't know if it's an inherent distrust from being born a New Yorker, or a cautious savvy cultivated after years of travel, but when people walk up close behind me, I get nervous and clutch my belongings tightly about my person.

I was in a Madrid restaurant, dining with two new Spanish friends, Ivan and Cristina, when a sixth sense alerted me to a presence hovering near my shoulder. A heartbeat later, I had managed to shift my backpack under the table with my left leg securely through an arm strap while simultaneously checking the four inside and outside pockets of my coat, which was hanging over my chair, and the back pockets of my pants.

Reassured that I was still in possession of everything I ought to be, I then looked over my shoulder, and froze. After all, it is animal instinct to freeze upon finding oneself caught in the glare of headlights. These particular ones originated from a pair of hideous green and pink plastic eyeglasses, which had flashlights affixed to each side of the frame, worn by a Chinese woman with an enormous leer on her face.

Slowly, my brain began to recognize other aspects of her appearance, such as the bobbing blue pseudo-alien antennae she wore on a plastic headband.

Three questions raced through my brain simultaneously:

1. How had she managed to escape from the asylum?
2. Were the security guards hot on her heels?
3. Why was she picking on me?

Something came flying at my face, and I jumped back, jostling the table and nearly spilling a bowl of gazpacho into Cristina's lap. Only afterward was my brain able to focus on the offending object, which resolved itself into a punching nun puppet replete with boxing gloves and wimple.

It had been ages since I had seen one of these relics of childhood, and before I realized what I was doing, I smiled.

It is a well-known fact of animal interaction that the baring of teeth is often interpreted as an indication of aggression, and the woman before me certainly seemed to interpret my smile as an invitation to parry. In the blink of an eye, she whipped around a tray she'd been hiding behind the back of my chair and thrust it under my nose.

The tray was filled with an assortment of kitsch: plastic doohickeys—figurines, change purses, rings—depicting licensed characters along the lines of Bart Simpson and recent Disney animated blockbusters; cheap gags; and cigarette lighters of diverse shapes and sizes, with bits that lit up.

I contemplated her arsenal, wondering what she planned to deploy against me next, when I finally understood that she was repeating "400" in Spanish. I pushed the tray away to indicate that I wasn't interested in buying anything. I wanted to return to my meal and the conversation of my friends. But I didn't trust this woman enough to turn my back on her.

> At my rebuff, the woman grabbed the crucifix around her neck and held it out in front of her, as if she mistook me for a vampire.

At my rebuff, the woman grabbed the crucifix around her neck and held it out in front of her, as if she mistook me for a vampire and was warding me off. She squeezed the arms of the cross and jets of flame shot out from Christ's head.

I couldn't resist. I bought four of the crucifix cigarette lighters as Christmas presents for friends back home.

Having at last managed to close a deal, the Chinese woman gave a predatory glance toward my two friends, who each shook their heads "no." She brandished her tray at us one last time, and then stalked toward new prey at the next table.

From this safer distance, I noticed that the woman had a plastic bag hanging in the crook of her elbow, filled with plastic-wrapped individual roses. I turned back to my friends and whispered, "What happened to the gypsy women here who used to sell roses and read one's future?"

"No way to compete with cheaper products out of Asia," Ivan said. "Welcome to the global economy."

"A pity," I said, tucking my new lighters into my backpack. "The *Gitanas* were far more ... authentic. Even if they were all supposed to be charlatans and pickpockets."

"If it'll make you feel any better," Cristina said, reaching across the table and grabbing my hand, "I've got gypsy blood somewhere in my family. Give me all the coins in your pocket, and I'll read your future for you."

Out of instinct, I declined.

LAWRENCE SCHIMEL *is a full-time author, anthologist and translator. He has published more than 70 books, including "Two Boys In Love" (Seventh Window), "The Future Is Queer" (Arsenal Pulp Press), and "Venus and Serena Williams" (Andrews Mcmeel). In collaboration with Spanish artist Sara*

Rojo Pérez, he has created numerous children's picture books, including "The Flying Pilgrim" (about the Camino De Santiago) and "Andrés Y Los Copistas" (about the Prado Museum). With Catalan artist Sebas, he created the comic "Vacation in Ibiza" (NBM Publishing).

Madrid to Toledo
Losing Juan
lisa d. tossey

Young, female, and traveling alone without any understanding of the native language, I took a last-minute opportunity to visit Spain, flew into Madrid's Barajas Airport, and secured a hotel room across from the city's Botanical Gardens on the Paseo del Prado, the wide thoroughfare stretching from the Estación de Atocha, in southeast Madrid, to the Plaza de Colòn, on its northern edge.

The capital of Spain is a bustling, modern city, but I had finished exploring most of its highlights on foot in 48 hours. What I really wanted to see were areas of Spain that were not so modernized. After reading an intriguing account of Segovia, a 2,000-year-old town of 60,000 just 90 kilometers northwest of Madrid, I decided to take a day trip there.

So about 8:30 the third morning, I left my hotel, consulted my map, and headed for the nearest bus station. It looked to be about 10 blocks away, in a residential section of the city. It was early in the morning on a weekday, a time when most American cities would be crowded with commuters making their way to work, but as I walked, I was struck by how empty the streets were. In the space of six blocks, I passed only two people; both were leisurely walking their dogs.

When I reached the corner where the bus station was supposed to be, there wasn't a bus to be found—or a station, for that matter. Instead, there was a large concrete shell that resembled a station, surrounded by construction equipment. Apparently, the publishers of my map were overly optimistic about the pace of construction here. Spotting a metro station across the street, I decided to make my way to the only other bus station shown on my map, on the opposite side of Madrid.

The Estación Sur de Autobuses was operating where promised, out of the basement of a large hotel. Relieved, I descended a long narrow staircase into the station and approached a ticket counter.

"*Autobus. ¿Un billete para Segovia?*" I attempted. The man behind the glass shook his head and muttered, "*No Segovia. Toledo.*" Confused, I tried again. Again, he shook his head and rattled off a stream of words, tapping his wristwatch with his finger. Then, realizing I was totally confused, he said, "*Autobus. Toledo. Diez minutos.*"

I retreated from the counter and dug a guidebook out of my daypack. It said that Toledo was 44 miles southwest of Madrid, in the Castilla-La Mancha region, and it described the city as "a place of drama and austerity, tinged with mysticism, that was long the spiritual and intellectual capital of Spain." Intrigued, I purchased a ticket and was on my way.

The bus deposited me at the foot of the walled city, leaving me to hike up along the outside to the twin turrets that supported the city's gates. As I passed through the foreboding entrance, I faced my first challenge: Which way do I go?

I consulted my guidebook, but even the most detailed map would be useless for such a maze-like town. Uneven cobblestone roads twisted up and down steep hills, barely wide enough for modern cars. Warrens of towering medieval stone buildings butted up against the streets. Overhead, intricate iron balconies, festooned with flowering plants in small terra-cotta pots, extended from the windows. This claustrophobic arrangement left little room for pedestrians. Four cramped streets branched out before me.

Then, Juan materialized. He was a small, well-dressed Spanish man in a brilliant blue silk shirt, black trousers and shiny black loafers. From his rapid Spanish and accompanying gestures, I gathered that he was offering to show me around the city. I shook my head and waved him away with a weak, "*No comprendo.*" He laughed and beckoned for me to come with him. Anxious, I spotted a large church off to my right and hurried toward it to seek sanctuary. Maybe I could get my bearings once I was inside. I walked through the wooden doors and heard the haunting chords of a pipe organ and a choir of voices. I paused at the interior doors, unsure if I should enter during a service. I turned to find Juan right behind me. He shook his head sternly, pointing toward the interior of the church, motioning that I shouldn't interrupt the service. I reluctantly followed him outside.

A cool breeze had begun to blow, bringing in thick gray clouds that promised rain. I turned onto the nearest road and started uphill. Juan was again at my side. I tried to ignore him, busying myself with finding the tiny umbrella that was buried in my pack. He pointed at a window here, a building there, talking constantly. I continued to climb, picking my way through the cobblestones.

Before long, he resorted to gesturing, bringing his hand up to his mouth as if he was eating. "*No*," I said, patting my belly to show that I was full—despite the fact that my stomach was rumbling from missing breakfast. He shrugged in response. I made a walking motion with my fingers, hoping to show that I just wanted to explore the city. He blew me a kiss in return. I quickened my pace.

It seemed that I had ventured into a residential area of Toledo. As in Madrid, the streets were void of people and cars. With Juan at my heels, I continued up the never-ending hill, hoping to come across a more populated tourist area. But the turns in the road and the towering buildings overhead made it impossible for me to find landmarks or gain a sense of direction. Juan became more forward, gluing himself by my side. His gestures grew increasingly obscene, and it dawned on me that he wanted to grab more than just a bite to eat. I decided to face facts and prepare for a worst-case scenario.

> **Juan became more forward, gluing himself by my side. I decided to face facts and prepare for a worst-case scenario.**

An Oprah Winfrey show on surviving dangerous situations flashed through my mind. Unfortunately, the part I recalled showed what do if you're locked in the trunk of a car—not the case here. I cursed myself for not paying more attention to the gospel of Oprah, and I reviewed my situation. First, I had to stay calm. I determined that, with my boots, I had a 6-inch height advantage over Juan and was in better shape physically, considering the way he was huffing up the hill next to me. I also had the trusty travel umbrella at my disposal. I clutched it tightly and lengthened my stride in an attempt to keep a few feet ahead of him.

As I was finalizing my survival plans, I heard voices coming from an alley on my left. I turned quickly, attempting to follow the sounds that were bouncing off the walls around me. To my relief, the alley opened onto a small plaza with three shops. I ducked into the closest one, a store displaying a wide array of silver jewelry. The lady behind the counter greeted me with a cheerful "*Buenos dias,*" and a wide smile. I smiled back, feigning interest in a rack of gaudy string bracelets. I could see Juan lurking outside the front window, so I browsed a while longer, looking over hand-tooled silver mirrors and delicate beaded earrings.

When I caught another glimpse of Juan's blue shirt outside, I scanned the shop and noticed a side door behind a rack of postcards. I walked over to open it, but it was locked. I pointed to the door and asked the shopkeeper, "*¿Por favor?*" She looked at me quizically. I spoke again with more emphasis: "*¿Por favor?*" This time, my desperation must have crossed the language barrier. She came over to unlock it. "*Gracias, gracias,*" I repeated as I rushed out the door backward. I was relieved to find a van parked at the entrance to the side alley, effectively blocking Juan's view of my hasty exit.

I quickly walked away, constantly looking over my shoulder for any sign of Juan. A few turns later, I entered a much larger plaza, filled with tourists, souvenir shops and cafés. It was a beautiful sight. Taking a few deep breaths to calm myself down, I retired into one of the cafés and found an empty stool at the far end of the bar. I refueled with *café con leche* and a croissant, keeping a wary eye on the plaza.

Half an hour and a few pastries later, my nerves began to settle. I had finally lost Juan. I ventured back out into the maze of Toledo, ready to lose myself again in Spain.

IN ADDITION *to getting lost in Toledo, Lisa Tossey has successfully lost her way in four other countries, the majority of the lower 48 states, and on her way home. When not staring hopelessly at a map, she has funded her travels by working as a flight attendant, bartender, Internet researcher, environmental educator and journalist. She lives in Maryland with her husband and their two road-tripping mutts, who remind her daily that every car ride can be an adventure.*

Valdelavilla
Talking My Way Into Spain

nicola escario

as a fanatical traveler of Spain, I thought I'd seen it all: flamenco, bullfights, sizzling beaches, endless nightlife, fiestas that include running to save your life or throwing a tomato to defend it. After two years of wanderlusting and traversing the peninsula, I considered myself an expert.

So there I was, in search of the next offbeat destination, yet convinced I'd left no Spanish stone unturned. If I hadn't been so rich on time and poor on income, I would have dismissed the intriguing travel offer that came my way. It sounded too good to be true:

> A week of accommodation
> in exchange for conversation!
>
> Wanted: English native speakers
> to spend 7 days in the Spanish countryside
> and converse with Spaniards who are
> in the process of learning English.

A beaming, multicultural group of faces on the poster invited me to join them to chat, play, walk, dine and wine with Spaniards against the beautiful backdrop of the local countryside, while Spanish-language company Vaughan Systems picked up the tab at either a 16th-century abandoned village, or a modern, four-star rural complex. The Spaniards, meanwhile, would get to improve their fluency in the quickest, most intensive manner possible.

It seemed like a win-win situation. I was, after all, looking for something different. And I could talk the hind leg off of almost anything. I decided that the best action to take was the impulsive one. Next thing I knew, I was signed up as an official conversationalist at an intriguing Spanish village. The only rule: No Spanish allowed.

My group of 20 fellow English-speakers consisted of Americans, Aussies, Brits, a sprinkling of Canadians and Irish, and a lone Kiwi. The lively bunch included everything from backpackers to retired CEOs, aged 21 to 80, our only common thread an irksome sense of curiosity that would make us fly halfway around the world to do something like this.

As we rode a bus winding down a narrow road into the valley of Valdelavilla, the last of civilization disappearing behind us, I noticed a pack of vultures flying above. Brian, the week's official Master of Ceremonies, informed us that, apart from being the only town within a 5-kilometer radius, Valdelavilla also was home to a vulture reserve. What was I getting myself into? I gripped the armrests and peered down into the valley. In the middle of the lush greenery, a cluster of rough stone houses and red-tiled roofs came into view.

When we Anglos (as they called us) arrived, we gawked at the narrow, winding cobblestone streets and the preserved 14th-century houses that made up the former sheepherder village. The low ceilings and wooden doors made us feel like giants in a fantastical medieval town. Then we started to notice people gawking at *us*. The women in our group from Oklahoma wore cowboy boots and hats, the Aussies wore board shorts, two men from Manchester sported loud Bermudas, and cameras hung around our necks.

The 20 Spaniards eying us, on the other hand, were affluent-looking business professionals, well-dressed, smiley and nervous. They spoke intermediate levels of English and had been sent by their companies to improve.

We fondly nicknamed them our "victims."

We started off with an icebreaker like musical chairs—except instead of chairs, we had Spaniards, and instead of music, we held conversations.

It started with talk about family and jobs. By Day 2, we'd moved to politics and religion, with the intellectuals in the group debating the Franco regime, and the more artistic ones discussing flamenco guitars and technique. We talked about everything from wine tasting to speed dating. The Texan ladies held a class on line dancing; the women from Sevilla on flamenco dance. Day 5 seemed to be officially declared existentialism day; on cue, everyone decided to ponder life's meaning. In the final days, we were all prompted to confess dreams and hopes, and share our most intimate secrets with strangers we knew we would probably never see again.

A typical day started with breakfast at 9 a.m., with two Spaniards and two Anglos per table. Round-robin conversations began at 10 a.m., with Spanish and English speakers paired off for hourly chitchat sessions, usually while exploring the countryside on a walk.

Lunch was served at 2 p.m., with more conversation over delectable three-course meals. Three to 5 p.m. was *siesta* time—officially declared the most important Spanish invention by mid-week. Afternoon activities included group games such as "Two Truths and a Lie" and Trivial Pursuit. During the day, Brian would discreetly pluck out innocent bystanders to rehearse some dizzily funny skits for entertainment that night. Dinner was served at 9 p.m., and still the chatting did not cease. It was intense and exhausting, but wonderful.

On the afternoon of the fifth day, as I walked with Patri, a yoga instructor from Galicia, I realized that her confidence had improved very much. This shy girl was now so chatty, I couldn't get a word in edgewise. Her English consisted of about 100 words that she deftly juggled around to get her point across, interrupted by a quick charade if confusion set in. The best thing about learning a language, she said, was that it opened doors to meeting people like us.

Antonio, sitting at my table, asked us how to say *idiota* in English. Easy, I told him; just drop the "a." Gumersindo, the group's official clown, helpfully offered five more synonyms. Antonio shouted off his newfound vocabulary to Pepe at the next table, and turned back, beaming. "This is a moment in history," he said. "One small word, one giant leap for language learning!"

> **We realized that smiles and nodding sometimes actually meant, "What the hell is he saying?"**

Half of the Spaniards got the joke; the other half looked puzzled but laughed and nodded anyway, a trick that proved most helpful during the week. We realized that smiles and nodding sometimes actually meant, "What the hell is he saying?" We also discovered that it wasn't vital for the Spaniards to understand everything. What they wanted was the courage to be able to express themselves in "real world" English when they traveled abroad.

The idea was that, since we spoke no Spanish and had no experience teaching English, the Spaniards would be more apt to use all five of their senses in the communication effort. Soon, the Spaniards found themselves blabbing away in English without having to stop, think and translate. And somewhere along the way, we all became friends.

There was Gumersindo, a guitar-playing, joke-cracking guy from the south of Spain. He taught us that making people smile could be a daily goal.

Antonio was an intelligent, sarcastic nut who liked racing motorcycles and made a living off Internet portals. He taught us that everything could be funny—all you have to do is open your mouth and laugh. "It's easy," he said, jabbing 80 year-old Scully in the ribs and sending her into fits of laughter.

Sweet Berta was a biologist who traveled the world to attend AIDS seminars, understanding about five sentences per conference. She taught me that a smile is worth more than a hundred words and is an excellent defense in moments of language crisis.

Luis taught me how to roll my "r's," Juan Carlos demonstrated the art of flamenco dancing, and Gustavo talked passionately about the Andalusian horse. Eva taught me that the phrase "Don't worry," when repeated after every two sentences, was the key to the stress-free Spanish lifestyle. But the best lesson for us Anglos was what *la vida española* really meant—to love life, to live for the moment, to truly feel alive.

My backpack and I traveled north to south in search of a way to explore both Spain and its people; to make that special trip that sideswipes you with an enriching human experience you'll never forget.

In that remote village deep in the heart of Spain, I found it. And all I had to do was talk.

NICOLA ESCARIO *is a freelance writer and full-time chocoholic. When not writing or chocolate binging, she enjoys flitting across the globe in search of the next unusual holiday. If you're up for an adventure as a volunteer conversationalist, project founder Richard Vaughan runs programs all year round. Applications are online at www.vaughantown.com.*

Pamplona

Running for the Boy

rachel sarah

"**h**ave you heard of the Running of the Bulls?" asked the young woman next to me as our train pulled out of the Barcelona station.

"It's in Pamplona, right?" I asked, recalling that I'd quickly passed over that chapter in my guidebook.

"Are you going?" she asked. Little did this stranger know that running with wild animals was so not me.

"No way. I'm an animal-rights activist." I had no interest in watching thousands of boys chase bulls over cobblestones.

"You don't have to run," she said.

"I'm sorry," I said.

She introduced herself as Leila and she looked about my age — I'd just turned 22 that summer — but man, I was more mature than her, for sure. I didn't believe in anything like bullfights or hunting. I was a vegetarian.

And I had my own plans. I'd just been awarded a scholarship for a summer writing workshop in Prague. I'd left my job as a reporter at a paper in New Milford, Connecticut, and flown to Europe, two weeks before classes were to begin. With just my heavily loaded backpack, I planned to reach Prague via Spain, where I'd check out all the museums and put my high-school Spanish to good use.

> **No one knew me here as that quiet girl from the suburbs who planned everything in advance. Maybe it would be good for me to let go a little.**

"We won't run with the bulls," Leila said. "We'll just watch."

I shook my head.

"This is the chance of a lifetime," she said. "We'll stay just one night and catch the bulls the next morning."

Maybe she just didn't want to be caught in the middle of a bull run alone. Her determination was working on me. Here I was, far away from home, in the land of flamenco dancing. Would one little night in Pamplona really spoil my plans? No one knew me here as that quiet girl from the suburbs who planned everything in advance. Maybe it would be good for me to let go a little.

We reached Pamplona after sunset. Drunken boys

staggered through the streets in white slacks and red sashes. They guzzled wine straight from the bottle, their shirts stained like blood. I looked away as they stopped at the corner and pulled down their zippers. Sleeping bags were strewn on the grass around Plaza de Castillo. A boy with bloodshot eyes strummed his guitar, singing in an Australian accent. A barefoot girl swayed at his knees.

We found the tourist center but were told that all the hotels had been booked months in advance. I broke out in a sweat as I realized that we'd have to pull an all-nighter. We turned another corner, onto Paseo de Hemingway, and we found ourselves in front of the bull plaza. This was too much for me. I didn't want to see any bloody bulls. I pulled on Leila's arm. "Let's go." I spotted a café across the street where we could relax and make a game plan.

Right there, in front of that café, is where I noticed him. The young man was standing on the opposite street corner, poised in the midst of all this dizzy red. I knew he was different. He wasn't a bullfighter. Even with the two-way boulevard separating us, I saw that this guy had large round eyes like an angel's. He was looking right back at me. My heart was pounding *get-him get-him*. I turned to my new friend and said, "I'll be right back—"

I didn't look both ways before crossing the street. My hiking boots carried me through the crowd. This wasn't like me. I never chased after boys. But I had to talk to him. I had to know who he was. Only he was turning around now. He was walking away.

Wait, wait— You've got to wait—

I pushed past people with my elbows. Finally, I caught up to him, out of breath, and tapped him on the shoulder. *Perdóneme*, I said. *¿Quieres tener una bebida?*

Oh, please. Sometimes I couldn't believe myself. Just listen to me, panting out the words "Do you want a drink?" As if I was offering him a sip from my water bottle. He looked at me kind of strangely, crossing his eyebrows. Then he said: *¿Porqué no?*

Why not? That meant "yes," didn't it?

We pushed our way back through the crowd. Now that I had him, I didn't know what to say. I pointed to myself: "Raquel."

Soy Gabriel, he said. We shook hands. I spotted Leila, who was sitting at a table. This was perfect. She already had a table. I waved to her. She waved back.

Soy bailarín, he said.

"You're a dancer?" I asked, to make sure I understood.

Contemporáneo, he said. This was perfect. He was a dancer. A modern dancer.

Estaba en un taller de baile el fin de semana, en este momento estuve regresando a—

I didn't understand. *¿Hablas inglés?*

"The English, I speak a little. Dance class end. I go home."

I shrugged my shoulders. *¿Casa?*

Mi casa está en Pamplona. He pointed down the street. So, his home was here. He was a native.

When we sat down with Leila, I looked straight at him. How do you know when the connection with another human being is authentic? You just know. He was like a playmate from my past. I knew him from somewhere. I didn't care if he came from some faraway corner of the world. I didn't care at all. I'd never felt this strongly about a stranger before.

He wasn't wearing any red or white like the bull runners around here. He wore a dark blue, hand-knit sweater, beige corduroys and leather sandals. He was short, like me, and he walked in this rhythmic cadence, gentle and soft. His hair was a wild array of curls. One lock hung down on his forehead. In this weird way, I thought, he almost resembled a bull.

"You stay in hostel?" he asked us.

I shook my head.

"My mother and father not in house," he said. "Come with me." He was pointing to himself.

Come home with him? But—

Suddenly, it was 3 a.m. What should we do? Leila and I whispered in English. My body said, Follow him.

Gabriel led us up the stairs to the first floor of a brick building on Avenida de Zaragoza.

As he searched for his keys, my friend nudged me. "He likes you," she said. I blushed.

Gabriel pointed to the second room down the hall, explaining that it used to be his sisters' room, but both of them were married now. There were two single beds, side by side, with clean sheets and lily-white throw pillows. My friend and I set our bags on the floor. I felt at home.

Buenas noches, he said. And just like that, he was gone, down the hall. I lay on my back in bed. But I wasn't tired. I couldn't get his eyes out of my head.

At sunrise, Leila was shaking me: "Get up. I think we've missed the bulls."

But I didn't care. I tiptoed down the hall, where a door was open. I stood there and admired Gabriel's steady breath, olive skin and soft brown curls. I took two steps into his room and touched his foot, light as a kiss. He lifted his head, startled.

I laughed. "We're going now. My friend wants to see the bulls."

He climbed out of bed and rubbed his eyes. He looked at his clock. "Late," he said.

It was eight o'clock. The bull run was starting right now. It would be over in a flash.

"You want coffee?" he asked.

"Yes." I would have said "yes" to anything for him right now.

"No," said Leila. "We have to get downtown. I'm sure we've missed everything."

We followed Gabriel into the hall and put on our shoes.

I leaned in the doorway, shyly. "Can I have your address?" I said.

He smiled and reached for a pen near the phone. I watched him write his name on a slip of paper. Then I pushed it into my back pocket.

On the steps, Gabriel bowed forward and gave me a Spanish kiss, his lips hardly touching my right cheek, then my left. I reached out and pulled him toward me, an American hug. Since he was just a couple of inches taller than me, our hearts met in the middle.

One summer later, I would return to Pamplona to marry him.

RACHEL SARAH *finally reached Prague and went on to report for The Prague Post from 1994 to 1996. Gabriel soon moved in with her. A year later, they got married at the Pamplona courthouse, not far from where they met. She is the author of "Single Mom Seeking" (Seal Press/Avalon).*

Pamplona
Crazy Girl
alicia jeanien salcedo-báez

It was 4:30 a.m., and all I knew was that something large had just fallen on my head, and I was freezing. As I struggled to unzip myself from my polyester cocoon, all I could think about was how I had gotten into this position, when I could have been safely tucked into a nice, warm bed.

Finally freed, I sat up to see a man and his drunken *compadres* stumbling around me, offering slurred Spanish apologies. *Lo siento, señorita!*

Actually, it was my behavior, not theirs, that was unusual. I was camped out on a patch of grass with my friend Natalie and two South African guys we had just met, attempting to sleep in the midst of thousands of revelers. We had all come together for *Los Sanfermines* and the *encierro*—the nine-day fiesta with the infamous daily running of the bulls.

My journey to the city of Pamplona and that little patch of grass had not been an easy one. Natalie and I had begun in Barcelona, not realizing that sheer masses of people would be trying to get to Pamplona at the same time. We'd waited in lines for hours at the train station, only to discover that we would not be departing as planned. This had led us to McDonald's—I am ashamed to admit—where we made three new friends, one guy from Australia and two from South Africa.

The Aussie, Jon, had run with the bulls that very morning. My eyes grew wide as I listened to his tale, and butterflies of panic rose in my stomach. He said women weren't common in the running, or particularly appreciated. Although I'm tall, at 5-foot-11, I am still a woman, and I didn't want to be worried about my welcome from the other runners. The bulls were more than enough to make me nervous.

Jon continued to talk: about the people he had seen hurt, about drinking nonstop, about enjoying the festival with all the other people in the city. The more I listened, the more I felt a machismo building up inside of me. I could definitely do this run, and beat out others in the process. I was going to take on all the bulls and I was going to emerge victorious!

I went off to the ticket counter and procured two seats on the first train out of Barcelona the next morning. A long ride through the Spanish countryside, with an old black-and-white movie crackling on the train's television, brought us to our destination. We stashed our large backpacks at the train station and filled smaller packs with essentials for the day.

A current of excitement rippled through the people at the station. Those on their way out of the city wore dirt-stained, triumphant faces, and clothing speckled pink from sangria. The fresh-faced travelers streaming off the trains replaced them happily.

Butterflies jumped in my stomach again, and I could hardly contain my excitement. Our first stop was to purchase official Pamplona gear—red scarves and white outfits necessary for the run.

> The air was so alive and everyone so joyous, I have never felt so insignificant and so important all at once.

I picked a scarf from the assortment on the table, and then knelt as the woman behind the table tied my scarf for me, inducting me with a kiss on the cheek and blessings from God to protect me.

It was official: I was really here, and I was going to run with the bulls. I felt invincible.

My new friends and I proceeded to the heart of the city, passing through increasing levels of noise and celebration, until we were engulfed by throngs of people singing, dancing and drinking in rhythmic motions that felt like ocean tides. The air was so alive and everyone so joyous, I have never felt so insignificant and so important all at once. On these narrow streets, cultures blended, and the thousands of people seemed to be enjoying this day as if it were their last. My nagging thought was that this might just be true. I joined in the merriment, but as day melted into night, I felt that the hours until the *encierro* could not pass fast enough.

Around midnight, Natalie selected a suitable patch of grass on which to catch a couple hours of sleep: a small island in the middle of a traffic circle in front of Club Cool. We zipped ourselves into our sleeping bags, and, soon after, the drunken man landed on my head, apologized profusely and wandered away.

As I zipped myself back up, feelings of apprehension seeped in. "I can't run with the bulls; that's crazy," I thought to myself. All of my bravado melted away, and I started shivering in my sleeping bag. What had I gotten myself into?

My cell-phone alarm went off at 6 a.m. Natalie and I dragged our weary bodies out of our sleeping bags and shivered in the morning air. To my surprise, there were still hundreds of people dancing and drinking from the night before. As we made our way to the starting line, I could hear sounds of laughter, but all I felt was fear. I started to tell Natalie that I just wanted to watch the run instead, but she looked at me as though I had sprouted an extra appendage.

"You were the one who convinced me to come here

and run! We came all this way, and you are not giving up. I don't care what you want to do, Alicia, you are running with me!" That was the end of that conversation.

We followed the mostly male crowd through the winding streets. The city looked so majestic and beautiful, I could hardly believe I was in the same place as the day before. The first place we picked to stand, we realized, was not only right in front of the gate where the bulls were released, it was also at the base of a steep hill. We moved to the top of the hill, where we met a bunch of American GIs and shared running strategy. Over the loudspeakers came announcements in multiple languages that this was the moment—and the last chance to leave the bull run.

Police officers came through the crowds, removing anyone who was drunk, and setting up barriers to keep the onlookers safe from the bulls and from us. Pamphlets on bull-running safety were distributed. Their advice, if you fell and were trampled, was to curl into a fetal position and protect your head at all costs. This advice offered little comfort to me. While I psyched myself up, the track was cleared. Natalie and I made a pact to meet up in front of the bullring, and we hugged for what could have been our last time. The first bell rang and I was off.

Natalie waited behind; she wanted to meet the bulls head on. I just wanted to live, so I went ahead, mixing in with the hundreds around me. When you run with a huge crowd, the only mission you have is to look out for yourself; there isn't time to think about anything else. The second bell rang to signal the release of the bulls, and chaos. I made it around the first dangerous turn OK, but near the second 90-degree turn, I was pushed into the crowds and thrown up against a wall. I looked around wildly for Natalie and spotted her running along as if it were her morning jog. I wanted to join her, but the two bulls right behind her held me back. When they passed, the men I was with pushed me out, urging me to run on.

Now I wanted to catch those bulls. What I didn't know was that the police had blocked off part of the road with a large wooden gate after the bulls passed. That trapped me with a large mass of people struggling to move. To my left, I saw one of the GIs I had met earlier, and neither of us could believe what had just happened. We didn't realize that another bell had rung, a second set of bulls was being released, and we had been herded for them to plow through. I made it to the other side of the gate.

Now I was on the most dangerous stretch of the run. Buildings on both sides of the street confined me to the narrow street. The bulls came up behind me. I stretched out my arm and tried to touch one, but it was out of my reach. With the threat of death or dismemberment passed, I began to search for Natalie. She was not among the casualties I saw along the way; she wasn't the person I saw being loaded onto a stretcher.

We found each other right in front of the ring.

She had narrowly missed getting trampled and almost made it into the stadium ahead of the bulls. We exchanged stories, enjoying a high like none we'd ever experienced. We had tempted fate and lived to tell the tale. As adrenaline coursed through my body, my only thought was, "Freaking awesome! Can we do it again?"

Natalie and I have since returned home. But in Pamplona, I became the crazy girl who ran with bulls—and I would do it again without a second thought.

ALICIA SALCEDO-BÁEZ *graduated from George Mason University with a B.F.A in photography and no has desire to become an adult just yet. She spent three months backpacking throughout Europe and is eagerly waiting for the day she can return. Her new goal in life is to see all seven continents, and she is hoping to find a job that will allow her to do just that (let her know if you have such a job). Alicia is trying to live her life to the fullest and experience all it has to offer, with no regrets.*

Fisterra, Galicia
The End of the World
eileen mckee

at some point in your life, after slogging through some dull periods and careening through some exciting ones, you start to wonder how far you'll go. How far you'll go professionally, or academically, or financially. Or, if you happen to be of the traveling breed, how far you'll go geographically. When I was 19, I went to the end of the world.

Fisterra—*Finisterre* is the Spanish translation—is a small but important site in Galicia, a proud province in the northwest corner of Spain. If you don't know your Latin root words, "*Finisterre*" is a compound of *finis*, meaning "end," and *terrae*, "earth." I spent six months in Galicia, based in the glorious city of Santiago de

Compostela, and was delighted to learn that the End of the Earth was a mere bus ride from home.

One drizzly Friday, armed with several chorizo sandwiches, a two-person tent and a couple of blankets, three friends and I set out to spend a weekend in Fisterra and experience the end of the world for ourselves.

Fisterra is the official end of the Camino de Santiago, the pilgrimage route that thousands make each year to venerate Saint James, whose remains rest in the cathedral in Santiago de Compostela. Though most pilgrims make it to Santiago de Compostela and stop, there are still some, the *peregrinos*, who continue the trek on foot for another week or so to Fisterra, satisfied with the knowledge that they can go no further.

The bus dropped us at the coast in midafternoon, and we wandered around the town, glistening gray in the characteristic Galician mist. Signs marked *Faro de Fisterra* led us out of the quiet streets and onto a wide coastal road. We hiked four across, occasionally snapping pictures of the dramatic cliffs in between pockets of fog. By the time we reached the *faro*, the lighthouse, we were tired, damp with the residue of the ocean, and eager for sandwiches.

Here and there, weary *peregrinos* rested next to their bulging backpacks. Then we saw a cloud of black smoke billowing around a corner, followed by a noxious whiff of something scorched and rubbery. We set down our packs and followed the smell. A middle-aged woman, bleached blonde and deeply tanned, stood next to what looked like a barbecue grill, gazing at the fog-obscured coastline and casually smoking a cigarette. She rested one foot on her backpack, and she was wearing thick hiking socks but no shoes. In fact, her *shoes* were the source of the black cloud and the tire-fire stink. They were apparently being barbecued.

"You're burning your shoes," my friend Trevor pointed out in Spanish. *"¿Por qué?"*

She smiled. "I've finished the Camino," she answered. "When you finish the entire thing, you burn the boots that brought you here and start life on a different foot." She exhaled a puff of smoke, looking relaxed. "It took me a year to walk the Camino. I started and stopped so many times, but now I am done, and I feel wonderful."

We congratulated her, then wandered around the base of the *faro*. The top of the lighthouse was swaddled in fog. Every few minutes, an earth-shaking noise blared from the foghorn. We scampered along the cliff in front of it, climbing gingerly over rocks and trying to get a proper view of the gray Atlantic in between the blasts. No wonder the Romans called this the end of the world, I thought, covering my ears just in time and feeling the noise reverberate in my chest. It was a sheer drop off the cliff to the ocean, with threatening rocks and angry waves crashing at the bottom: *Costa da Morte*, the coast of death.

Eventually we packed up and continued our trek, looking for a place to camp out, eat, drink and be merry. We waved goodbye to the bootless woman and found our way to a fire road that led us up into the hills of Fisterra. The fog now hovered high above us, not penetrating the thick canopy of trees. It was much quieter here. The crashing waves and the blast of the foghorn were faint in the distance.

We found a small clearing off the road, near an old rock wall that seemed to run throughout the forest. It was perfect—not too far from the main road, cozily surrounded by stately trees, and with plenty of rocks for making a fire pit. Maybe we were trespassing, but apparently we weren't the first: here and there, bits of trash were scattered, along with a few empty shotgun shells.

"Well," I said, "at least we know people have camped here before."

Kevin, exploring over bushes and high grass, suddenly stopped. "Look at this," he said, pointing to a small sapling in a cleared area. "What *is* that?"

It appeared to be a dried, shriveled chicken foot, dangling on a blue string from one of the branches. We stopped and stared. Some kind of end-of-the-world voodoo? We stood in the quiet clearing uneasily for some time, weighing our options, until we finally decided that, perfect campsite or not, a voodoo chicken foot and empty shotgun shells were bad signs in a place where we planned to sleep.

Back to the road. The higher we hiked into the hills, the less hospitable the woods became; the soft pine-needle carpeting gave way to wilder sticks, branches and rocks. Maybe a single dried chicken foot wasn't so threatening after all.

As we retraced our steps to the clearing, we heard voices up ahead. From our turnoff to the clearing, we saw three young hikers meandering along the road.

We dumped our backpacks on the ground and stretched. The hikers reached the turnoff for the clearing, and then stopped. We watched them as we unpacked our remaining sandwiches. They appeared to be discussing where to camp, just as we had not half an hour before. Finally they turned and walked toward us into the clearing, hesitantly at first.

> Maybe a single dried chicken foot wasn't so threatening after all.

"*Hola*," we greeted them. They *hola*-ed back politely. With backpacks, heavy-duty hiking boots, and bandannas tied around their heads, they appeared to be *peregrinos*. In Galicia, when you encounter a *peregrino*, it's often a tossup as to what language to use; it is not rare to encounter English, German or French.

We stood in the clearing and sized each other up. It took only a moment before one of the hikers, probably noticing our baseball caps and Nikes, asked us in perfect English, "So—are you guys camping here, too?"

Soon we were helping them clear space for their sleeping bags and tent, pointing out the shriveled chicken foot and giggling. Our group of four had now become a group of seven. The three hikers, two Canadian guys and a French girl, were finishing the Camino, taking their time on the last leg of their journey. We handed Kevin and the two boys some money and sent them into town to buy a few bottles of wine and more food. The rest of us took charge of building a fire.

The rock wall was a perfect backdrop for a campfire. Trevor and I gathered large stones from the crumbling end and arranged them in a circle, then went to help our friend Stacy and the French girl collect firewood and twigs.

After the dried chicken foot and shotgun shells, Trevor and I weren't surprised to come across a single rotting door lying nearby, the doorknob and hinges still intact.

"What on earth happened here?" I asked no one in particular. "How would a *door*—shotgun shells—that weird foot thing—" I shook my head, bewildered. "Where *are* we?"

"We're at the end of the world," said the French girl gleefully. "Where else?"

The mysterious rotting door made excellent firewood. Soon, we had a respectable campfire blazing. The French girl brought out a pot, filled it with water, and started making coffee. I perched on a nearby boulder with my sketchbook, feeling pleasantly content. We sat around and chatted, sharing stories about where we had been and people we had met.

As darkness fell, Kevin and the guys returned with

several bottles of cheap Spanish *vino tinto*, plastic cups, a loaf of crusty bread and a hunk of *queso gallego*, delicious local cheese.

Something about a campfire inspires camaraderie. Maybe it's because there's no way to comfortably sit around one and stay warm without getting close to your neighbor. Or maybe it was just the fresh coastal air and the wine, but soon our motley crew was laughing and joking as if we had known each other all our lives. This is what traveling is supposed to be, I thought. Meeting different people, sharing stories and wine and good conversation. When you travel, there are no strangers, only friends you have yet to meet. One of our *peregrinos* had spent a year in the military, until he got kicked out and bought a one-way ticket to Germany, living on his own from city to city ever since. The other talked politics with the knowledge of a CIA agent, giving impromptu history lessons on Basque nationalism. The French girl was full of colorful stories of the *albergues* and other hikers on the Camino.

That night, after the fire had died down and the wine bottles were empty, we crammed four tipsy people into a two-person tent. I settled down with my forehead mashed into Stacy's side and my feet resting against Kevin's back, thinking hazily about *peregrinos*, the bootless woman, our three new friends, the various exhausted hikers we'd seen on the road to the *Faro de Fisterra*. The end of the world was a strange place. The rocky cliffs, the velvety fog, the weathered lighthouse—

they were quietly constant, unchanging. The people and history swirled about them, coming and going, as they had been for centuries.

Here I was, a sort of *peregrino* myself. We're all on a journey of some sort, aren't we? And although I wasn't exactly sure of my destination, I couldn't help feeling confident in my general direction. I could be happy if this was as far as I'd ever get—but I knew it wouldn't be, and that made me happier. I'd reached the end of the world, and the beginning. I drifted off to sleep, to the low, rumbling blast of the foghorn.

EILEEN MCKEE *graduated cum laude from the University of Richmond in 2006 with a B.A. in Spanish and psychology, and a minor in studio art. She hopes to pursue a career in art therapy. Eileen is constantly scribbling in a sketchbook, and she acquired an expert's taste for bagpipes and kalimocho while in Galicia.*

Camino de Santiago
To Be a Pilgrim
mara ginnane

the wind whips around me, shoving me off course and flapping my jacket wildly against my arms. My heavy backpack, tightened around my hips and shoulders, pulls me toward the ground. On both sides of the road, groves of poplar trees bend and shake with every gust, hurling leaves and small branches in all directions. Above, dark clouds boil and swell, full to bursting with the threat of rain.

This is my worst day yet. Three-hundred kilometers into an 800-kilometer trek across Spain, I am wishing I had never heard of the Camino de Santiago. My tired legs strain to propel my body forward on blistered feet, and my eyes squeeze nearly shut, tearing up against stinging sand blown by the roaring wind. I had been hiking with three companions, but they have fallen behind now. I can't even hear the crunching of their boots on the gravel road.

For the last half-hour, I have been trudging forward, seemingly on my own. Angel, the gay Spanish-born German philosopher; Willan, the quirky 18-year-old Englishman; and my gutsy college friend, Heather, are struggling, too. Heather developed a chronic, searing pain in her right knee, Angel is trying to stave off tendonitis in his left ankle, and Will had to stop at a hospital to treat his infected blisters.

Some people we met became too injured to continue walking, and they hired taxis to drive them to each town so they wouldn't fall behind their groups of pilgrims. We considered any use of non-ambulatory transportation cheating. We'd risk permanent injury rather than not make it to the day's destination on our own two feet. One morning I woke up with a severe stomach flu, yet I staggered on, vomiting every 20 minutes. Our lives had only one purpose now: to place one booted, aching, blistered foot in front of the other. This is the creed of us pilgrims on the Camino de Santiago.

A month before, from the comfortable safety of my own home, it had seemed like a great idea to begin my seven-month stay in Spain with a trek from the mountains of the Basque country to the holy city of Santiago de Compostela.

This small city in Spain's northwest corner, the supposed resting place of St. James, was one of the most important cities to Catholicism after Jerusalem and Rome. For centuries, this trek had been the most famous journey in Christianity, equivalent to the Muslims' pilgrimage to Mecca.

Part of what drew me was its spiritual nature. I had just started opening up to the possibility of God, and, growing up with no religion whatsoever, I was fascinated by the trek's history and mystical tradition. Just out of college with a nearly useless degree, I saw that this path had roots. It had purpose. And it promised to make me a pilgrim, whatever that meant.

But, the Camino is more a tourist attraction today. Not a single person I had walked with up to this point had brought any religious motivation to it. Instead, I found myself with atheistic, cynical and altogether irreverent people—wonderful friends and entertaining company, but they found ponderings on God not only laughable but sometimes disgusting.

At the same time, the trek was loaded with religious artifacts. We must have stopped in 50 churches and cathedrals so far, from abandoned stone structures to world-famous, big-time cathedrals like Burgos, which we visited this morning.

A huge, grey mass of spires, Burgos houses more gilded opulence than I could fathom. Staring up, open-mouthed, at the white, vaulted ceilings and pillars carved with a thousand cherubs, I wondered at the sheer quantity of wealth, resources and labor that had gone into this building. What was the purpose of it all? What happened to the message of simplicity and compassion the man they worshiped had given his life to demonstrate? It must have been built to inspire awe of the glory of God, but what I felt was amazement at the greed of mankind and the waste of all this wealth on a building, while millions were starving and dying.

I felt confused and disgusted as we left Burgos. It was 2 p.m., and we still had 19 kilometers to cover to reach the next town before dark. By 3 p.m., thunderheads were closing in on us, and we wondered if starting so late was such a good idea. In the next half-hour, the situation worsened dramatically. Now I find myself ahead of the others, cut off from them by the violent air, focusing with all my might on the task at hand: to move forward.

Eight-hundred kilometers in 30 days works out to 27 kilometers—almost 17 miles—per day. After 16 days, my body has adjusted to carrying the heavy pack, my legs have grown stronger, and I have learned how to care for my blisters by threading them with iodine-soaked string. I also begin to realize that this constant pain, pounding up through the bones of my feet into my knotted shoulders, will be as much a part of the trek as the dry ham sandwiches we choke down daily from the small-town bars that dot the trail.

After a few hours of walking, my feet become sort of numb. On a good day I am able to disconnect from my body, allowing it to carry me across the Spanish *meseta* while my mind wanders on a different plane.

I look up from the rocky ground, from my mud-caked boots and six-days-dirty pants, toward the thrashing treetops, the distant horizon, the steely sky, the angry clouds. I feel so small, so powerless, so insignificant in this landscape.

The wind gusts and I stumble to the side, throwing out one arm to keep my balance. How did I ever think I could conquer this distance? How did I imagine I had some control over what happened to me out here? To the wind, I am nothing but a bit of carbon to be toyed with: ushered gently onward or picked up and smashed open like an oyster on a rock.

The power of nature overwhelms me and I feel my breath catch in my throat. I feel everything I know drain away, leaving me naked, vulnerable, and suddenly terrified.

The power of nature overwhelms me and I feel my breath catch in my throat. I feel everything I know drain away, leaving me naked, vulnerable, and suddenly terrified. Panic rises up within me, but I push it down with a hard swallow. I close my eyes and continue forward, giving myself up to the wind, sending my thoughts skyward, and I cannot help but pray—an act that usually feels foreign but now seems the only recourse.

"Dear God, guide me and help me to know the right path. Keep me safe from the bitterness and shallowness

I see so much of in the world. Help me to love freely and without fear. Give me the strength necessary to live every day with compassion. Help those whom I love to do the same. In these and all things, guide me." The words are lifted from my mouth and carried off on the wind, and I feel myself become lighter with their leaving.

I think I am finished, but more sound floats up and out of my mouth in a high, rich reverberation. I sing hallelujahs to the sky, harmonizing with the wind, the melody seeping from my throat like honey. I lift my arms out to my sides, letting them ride the wind, and I find it helps me balance. Suddenly, I no longer feel small and insignificant, a rowboat tossed about in an angry sea. Rather, I am filled with a light that tingles in my core and makes me feel strong with hope. In this moment, God becomes absolutely real to me.

I push onward with my face turned up to the heavens, carried on by the wind, or in spite of it, and my hair, yellow like straw, whips about my face like the trees whip over the fields. I am part of this place in all its chaos and fury and beauty and power. My legs stride certain and strong beneath me, and I delight in the ability of my body—my tiny, flawed, imperfect body—to propel me forward in such a tempest. I do not turn to check behind me for my companions, because, to my surprise, I am enjoying this feeling of utter solitude.

An hour later, I stop and wait for my friends to catch up. My legs feel weary again, but my spirits are still high, and I am thrilled with the day. Heather is the first to plod up to me, gripping her walking stick tightly in one hand, cheeks red with windburn.

"I hate this f---ing wind," she says, stamping her stick into the ground for extra emphasis. "I was screaming at it back there: 'Bring it on, you bastard!'"

"Think it heard you?" I ask, a bit stunned at her vehemence.

"I don't f---ing know. I just hate it."

Angel and Will walk up then, faces grim, hats pulled down over their ears. Angel says nothing, and I know this is a bad sign. Will smiles briefly, which for someone so hyperactive and overly dramatic is akin to a fierce frown.

"You two all right?" I ask.

"Let's just keep going and get out of this miserable wind," Angel spits out in his slight German accent before pushing past me. I look questioningly at Will.

"Neveh betteh," he says in his British lilt, giving me his perennial answer whenever anyone asks how he is doing. "But this wind is a bit of a wanker, eh?"

We all continue walking, but for the first time I feel distant from these people I have shared so much with. They are fighting the wind, battling against nature, bitter and angry and frustrated at the world, while I am feeling euphoric in my peace with it. In this moment, I understand that a chasm has formed between us, and I am surprised to realize I would not cross over to their side for anything.

My entire approach to life has changed. I know

now that I can go 36 days with no make-up, two sets of clothes, and no razor. More deeply, I feel respect for my body: I have walked 800 kilometers and kept going when I thought I would collapse. I've developed amazing friendships that have taught me more than I could have imagined.

Even more deeply, the Camino finally enabled me to open to the sacred—to prepare space for it in my cluttered and self-absorbed mind. I will strive to keep my heart open to all that comes my way, and to see beauty in it all. I have only to think back to the light that surged through me on the *meseta* to feel strong again and full of hope. Whenever I fear I have lost my way, I know now that with every step, I will find help. I must only ask. And that is the greatest lesson of the Camino: A true pilgrim is never really alone.

MARA GINNANE *grew up in the red-rock country of Moab, Utah, and no, she is not Mormon. After returning from Spain, Mara moved to Tallahassee, Florida, where she can experience the thrill of a different world within her own country. Apart from alligator wrestling and red-neck watching, she will be pursuing her master's degree in American Studies at Florida State University.*

TARJETA POSTAL

There is nothing
like the pity
of being blind
in Granada.
- Francisco de Icaza

Andalusia

Castiñeiras

What I Learned About Coleoptera By Having a Few Climb Up My Shorts

mike riley

We pulled off of the cobblestone road near Castiñeiras, and drove between the sand dunes onto a wood-chip road that cut through a field of knee-high weeds down to the beach. As Alberto drove, I planned out how I'd shoot my photographs. "The sun is setting fast and I want some good shots from the top of the dunes," I told him. "We gotta hurry. Real *rapido* like."

Alberto grunted, more concerned about not

breaking the two chilled bottles of wine clinking against each other in the back. Tins of anchovies, crumbly cheese and a long loaf of bread would complete our dinner, which we planned to enjoy on the beach. They filled the car with a dry and peasant-like odor.

"As soon as we stop, I'm gonna run up the dunes, take some shots. I'll meet you at the beach. You bring the food."

The car slowed. I jumped out before it stopped and ran through the field of weeds toward the dunes. Clods of sand and wood chips flipped up and hit me on the back and chest.

"Oiiii!" I heard Alberto yell behind me. I ignored him, which I usually do whenever he talks. "Aiiii!!!" Alberto yelled. His voice was faint through the loud waves and humid air.

I ignored him again as I reached the dunes, huffing and puffing. I draped my shirt on my back and began climbing on all fours. The sun slid behind the sand mountain; I started to panic and climbed harder. My muscles yelled, my lungs stretched, my heart pounded. I slipped, got a mouthful of sand, continued climbing. Sand scraped between my teeth as I tried to breathe. It coated my tongue and irritated my mouth. My girlfriend came to mind. "I gotta get rid of her," I thought.

Heaving and gasping, I reached the top of the dune. The sun was dim, beautiful, imposing. I pulled my camera from my sweaty side and shot my photographs as the sun dropped. I took some photos of the Atlantic with the sun in the right corner of the frame, then turned to shoot more and stopped. "What the...?" I mumbled.

Fact #1: Absurdity of cursing is directly proportional to the number of Coleoptera up your shorts.

I lowered my camera and watched Alberto. He was by the car, at the bottom of the dunes, running in tight circles in the middle of the wood-chip lane, his arms flailing like a Michael Jackson video in fast-forward, ripping his shirt off and swinging it over his head like a poorly trained stripper. He cursed—partly censored by the wind and waves—in Spanish: "... Crap on you and the milk of the mother of all dogs ... !"

"Odd!" I thought.

I lifted the camera and continued snapping. I heard more cursing and looked down; Alberto was rolling on the ground frantically, kicking up tufts of sand, swatting at something.

"Holy virgin and thirty muddied hosts!" Alberto yelled.

"Strange!" I thought.

I decided I had taken enough pictures, so I turned and ran down the dunes in long, careless bounds.

Alberto yelled. He was running through the knee-high weeds, the sun setting over the dunes, casting a red glow over the beach toward me. If Alberto were a girl, it would have seemed romantic, but it was Alberto, and he was sweaty and chunky and cursing like a Folsom Prison inmate in a foul mood—and so it was, frankly, a bit gross.

"¡¿Qué pasa?!" I yelled. "What's up?!"

Alberto ran, his face turning left and right frantically, his eyes terror-wide, his arms swinging high. He reached the edge of the weeds and ran off the wood-chip path onto the beach. His gaze changed from terror to confusion. He looked back at where the reeds ended and the sand began. Then he walked toward me, shaking out his shirt. He put his shirt back on, then reached up his shorts and began feeling around his underwear.

"Yikes! Pervert!" I mumbled. I noticed he had not brought the food, and it angered me. The sun was low, and if we wanted to eat on the beach, we did not have much time. "Where's the food?!" I yelled.

"O, just-a sut up! Just-a sut up!" he yelled back, obviously distressed.

"¿Qué pasa?" I asked. Alberto shook his head and clarified in Spanish. "¡Plaga!"

"Plague?"

"Back dere!" Alberto pointed to the car.

"What's back there?!"

"Plague!"

I stomped off to let Alberto know what I thought of his plague, of his love handles, of his not bringing the wine so I could wash the sand out of my mouth.

"I tell you!" Alberto warned.

I grunted and stepped off the beach, onto the wood chips and into the weeds. Then I heard them. It started as a light hum, gentle like a harmonica. The hum grew into a buzz—louder, angrier, edgier—as black dots shot up from the sand, darting left and right.

Fact #2: Intensity of yelling is directly proportional to the number of Coleoptera on your body.

"I tell you!" Alberto yelled. "That just-a them!"

We were surrounded. One of the dots zigged left and zagged right, fumbled in the air, and crash-landed on my arm with a small thud.

"What the—!" I yelled. A shiny black beetle, an inch long, with thick pincers and thin legs pushed its way up my arm. I tried to say something witty and memorable, like, "Alberto, your girlfriend just dropped in!" but managed only, "Uhhh…"

Alberto gasped and screamed, "Uuuuu-aaah, one in my shirt!" He cursed in Spanish, "Confound the mind of the mother of everything born in this holy town!"

I turned, pointed and began laughing at Alberto's predicament: "Ha, ha! You got a beetle crawling into your love handles! You better watch it isn't crushed by your…uh, ah, oh. …" A beetle crawling into my shirt interrupted me. "Ah … aaaaah … AAAAAH!" I yelled.

The swarm of beetles thickened into a cloud, then a billow, then a plague. They buzzed around us, curiously landing, exploring. They flew erratically, colliding into us constantly, irritated we had stepped on their breeding ground.

Fact #3: Coleoptera live and breed among wood chips. Side facts: Coleoptera do not mind sweaty underwear. Also, they are perverts.

"Whoa, whoa, wait! Hey, don't go there!" I yelled at the beetle crawling up my leg. He went there. I felt tickling and crawling where there should be no tickling and crawling. My yelling reached notes higher than I knew existed. The beetle and his friends scampered, romped, scuttled in my shorts.

"Ai! Ai! Ai!" Alberto yelled. "AIIIII!!!!" He screamed like a plaid-skirted schoolgirl.

We ran. Running kept them out of our shorts; we ran as fast as we could. Alberto ripped his shirt off and swiped it above his head as he ran. I did the same. We yelled more.

"Aaagh!" Alberto cursed in Spanish. "May your insect mothers find out their husbands are virgins!"

We weighed our options; running kept the bugs off, but running away from the car seemed counterproductive. So we ran around the car. Our legs burned and our lungs stretched. Our love handles jiggled, our man-boobs bounced; sweat drops dangled from our noses. We slowed. The beetles landed on our heads and chests. They rappelled into our shorts.

"What we do?!" Alberto yelled.

"I don't know!" I yelled back, scraping a beetle off my head. "What's the car like?"

"¡Muchos! ¡Muchisimos!"

I looked in the window. A large group of disoriented beetles had flown in through the open passenger-side window and were bouncing into glass and seats, unable to find their way back out. I groaned.

"Open door!" Alberto yelled.

"Good idea!" I said. More beetles, attracted to the dome light, swarmed in.

"Holy Mother of Spain and hater of all beetles!" Alberto yelled in Spanish.

I slammed the door shut before more could get in and looked at Alberto. We were tired, and our distress was obvious on our faces. The beetles grew bolder as we slowed down.

> We were tired, and our distress was obvious on our faces. The beetles grew bolder as we slowed down.

"We gotta get out of here!" I wheezed. "¡Vamonos!"

Alberto nodded his head emphatically. We opened the car doors and jumped in, onto seats crawling with beetles, shuddering as Alberto jammed the key toward the ignition, missed, missed, and missed again.

"Come on!" I yelled.

I felt the beetles crawling underneath me and in my shorts; I pinched my butt cheeks. Alberto yelled and grew a sudden inch in height; I guessed an exceptionally curious *Coleoptera* had found a new path.

"¡Vamos!" I yelled again.

Alberto found the ignition, slammed the gears into reverse, backed up, slammed on the brakes, shot forward. We sped down the wood-chip road, swatting at beetles, digging them out of our shorts and chest hair, yelling and shivering.

We rolled down the front windows and watched the whipping wind toss the beetles in its current, twirling them until they hit the rear windshield of the hatchback, where they were pinned against the glass.

Fact #4: Coleoptera in your shorts will drive you to violence and unexplained crying.

Alberto and I recognized our chance. I bunched up my shirt and threw it behind me so it hit the back window. "Ha! Ha!" I laughed a crazed and evil laugh, like a villain in a B movie. Alberto caught on and his eyes narrowed. "Killem!" he shouted, his voice laced with insanity and excitement.

I pulled off a shoe and threw it against the pinned beetles. It felt good. I pulled off the second shoe and threw it, too.

"Ha! Ha!" Alberto laughed. He handed me more to throw: CD cases, a book, his shirt. "Ha ha!" he screeched.

I lunged back over the passenger seat, reached over the backseat and pushed open the hatchback; the wind drew through the car and cleansed the back window of the beetles—disappeared, gone, *adios*.

The next few days of our Spanish road trip were nervous ones. Whenever we saw a leftover beetle in the car, we slammed it with a shoe until it became pulp. The back seat was a beetle battlefield. We shivered at odd times, for no reason. Whenever we saw the other shiver, we reached into our pants and made sure *Coleoptera* had not nested in a new warm and cozy home.

One time, I reached behind Alberto's driver seat, and my sleeve accidentally brushed his ear. He jumped, yelled, swatted at me and insulted me. I thought he was going to cry, shake and crawl into the fetal position.

He should have. I would have. It happens to people who know too much about *Coleoptera*.

MIKE RILEY *is a magnet for awkward situations. Do not travel with him. He now lives in Central Asia, where awkward situations have become a part of daily life. He is busy learning the local languages and hopes to study a bit of the literature. Mike loves international soccer, hiking and literature. However, he loves his wife more. Isn't he a great guy?*

Nerja
Miguel's Bar
halldór örn gunnarsson

I've walked past this place a couple of times before. Old guys sit in there drinking, and it seems to be a bar, even though there's no sign indicating that it is. It is on a small street in the town of Nerja, on the southern coast of Spain. The street is lined with white houses, and it's so narrow that people who park their cars on it fold their side mirrors flat when they park, so the mirrors won't be broken off by passing cars.

One day, after gathering up the courage, I walk in. I hadn't come here before because I wasn't sure I'd be welcome. It just seemed to be a rather private, local place. Also, I stand out. I'm paper white, I'm 6-foot-3, and I don't speak Spanish.

I duck to get through the door. It's a bar all right, and I feel at ease immediately. My worries were unfounded.

The room is about four meters wide and six meters long. It smells of cigarettes. There is a television in the corner to the left of the entrance, and when you look at it, you can see the street reflected on the screen. So that explains why I always felt the old-timers were looking at me when I walked past.

I sit down at the bar. The bartender moves quickly and has a joyful way about him. He is short, stocky and bald, and he wears a green wool vest over his white shirt. His name is Miguel.

"*Uno cerveza, por favor,*" I say, using almost the whole extent of my Spanish knowledge.

"*Sí, claro,*" Miguel says. As he opens the fridge, the plastic door of the inner freezer compartment falls off onto the floor. Miguel laughs in embarrassment, and I try to laugh with him. The only other customer, Antonio, is unfazed. He just gives me a look that tells me: "He always forgets about that damn freezer door. It's been like that for weeks." I smile back at him, a smile that I hope conveys, "*Sí,* I know the type."

Antonio is wearing all black. He looks about 70 years old, but he might be 80. Anyway, he looks too old to give a damn, and that makes him mysterious to me. As I turn around, Miguel is standing there with two types of beer. He asks me which one I would like.

"Cruzcampo," I say, forgetting the "*por favor,*" which

I instantly feel bad about. He opens the Cruzcampo, puts the other one in the fridge, and uses the opportunity to fiddle with the plastic door a little. I ask him how much for the beer; he says, "*Ochenta centavos, o noventa con patatas*" and holds up a bag of potato chips. I give him one Euro, and he pours a few chips onto a saucer on the bar table. He hands me the salt, so I can salt them myself.

The beer is the perfect temperature. "This guy knows what he's doing," I think. I take a nice long swig and look around. There are lots of religious symbols in the bar, balanced by old, sun-bleached posters of nude women. This place is so modest and straightforward that I can't help loving it.

> This place is so modest and straightforward that I can't help loving it.

The three of us turn to watch the lottery ladies on the television screen. Three generations of men, from two countries, I think, but we don't have a language barrier when we're watching the lottery. Miguel and Antonio have both bought tickets, of course, because that's what you do if you're Spanish. Nobody wins anything. Miguel rips his ticket and speaks to me in Spanish as he reaches for an old lottery ticket that he has saved. He explains to me that he had been only one number from winning the big one. He has written the right number on the ticket above the wrong one.

Antonio has heard this story so many times that

he goes and sits down at a little table in the corner. The ticket is from 1989. "A close one," I say in English. Miguel looks blank, so I move my hand up to my eye and look through the tiny space I form between my thumb and my index finger. Miguel understands this and smiles. He is missing his two front upper teeth, but he has an amazingly warm and real smile. I smile back, and I order another Cruzcampo, not forgetting the *"por favor"* this time. Miguel zips over to the fridge and opens it carefully. I move over to the corner, because I want a better viewpoint and I don't like to sit close to the TV. It's hard enough for me to understand what's going on without the TV blaring in my ear.

Two more old-timers walk into the bar.

Miguel brings me my beer and takes some time explaining that his dad, "bless his memory," was born in the same year that they started brewing Cruzcampo. He says all of this while clutching his hands together as if in prayer. Well, here's to your dad, I say, smiling, and I raise the bottle to take a drink. Miguel gives me a blank stare, and then decides to smile it off, too. I give him two Euros and tell him to keep the change. Miguel is reluctant to accept my tip, as tipping isn't customary in Spain. But after some persuasion, he accepts the change. He puts it in a little blue can on the shelf of the bar.

"*Para los niños*" he says, and he shows me a worn picture of five children. "*Sí, para los niños,*" I say. Are they yours? "*No, no,*" Miguel says, asking one of the newcomers to explain to me that these are orphans in Malaga. "Miguel is not married," a slick-haired lawyer says, and Miguel shakes his head approvingly. "Thanks," I say to the lawyer, who speaks better English than he gives himself credit for. Miguel bolts over to the fridge to get beer for the newcomers. He forgets about the freezer door again, and it crashes to the floor. He throws his hands up in the air and swears: "*Hijo de puta.*"

Everybody else can't help laughing, and Miguel smiles again, a little embarrassed. Antonio just shakes his head.

HALLDÓR ÖRN GUNNARSSON *is an Icelandic photojournalist. He is a recent graduate from Western Academy of Photography in Victoria, British Columbia. Halldór finds inspiration to travel in everything from books to a slice of pie. He currently resides in Western Canada.*

Costa del Sol

Spain Without a Backpack

elliott dykes

Peter picked up two hitchhikers from Scandinavia, probably just to make Heather mad. I was sitting in the back seat, chewing on chorizo and wishing I had a bottle of wine. Peter revved up our rented subcompact—now packed with two sweaty hitchhikers, two old friends, and one whiny chick—and resumed barreling south down the Costa del Sol.

When we stopped for gas, Heather told Pete to ditch the hitchhikers. I didn't really want them, either. The three of us were crammed in the back seat, pressed against the windows, and they needed a bath.

We dropped them on the side of the road in the dark.

In retrospect, that wasn't a nice thing to do. I have no idea where they could've gone. But they seemed happy. I, on the other hand, was tired and cranky, and we still had nowhere to sleep for the night. I should've picked up a bottle of wine, I thought. I could've spared the two bucks. I sat in the back seat and tried to imagine what would become of the hitchhikers.

Our plan had been to rent a car and drive down the coast of Spain, from Barcelona to Granada. We would park in the evenings at a beautiful spot and camp under the stars, cooking over a small fire and sipping cheap red wine until we'd solved the world's ills. The next day, we'd do it again. It was a good and noble plan.

But the first night, the highway didn't run next to the ocean. We could see it in the distance, reflecting the moonlight, but there was never a connecting road. So we turned down a farm road, a wild goose chase that left us sleeping in a farmer's field.

The next night, we got drunk with a group of travelers from Germany, at a very cute and remote bar right on the coast. The bar owner said we could leave our car at his place and camp on the beach. That was a terrific stroke of luck, until we woke up at 5 a.m. in the rain, a river running under our tent.

Heather was always grumpy in the mornings; she said she couldn't function without an espresso and a croissant. I was grumpy that morning, too—thanks to too much alcohol, no sleep, and the fact that everything I owned was wet.

So I figured we were due a good night. We passed Alicante, and the coastline rose to a cliff overlooking the sea at La Villa Joyosa. The weather was crisp and dry, the sky cloudless. My stomach was empty. I felt a far-off, romantic stillness.

Peter found a great spot that night. We watched the moon rise over the Mediterranean, revealing currents like silver hair over the water. We drank wine and ate *embutidos* and felt very good about ourselves.

Soon, we were best friends, despite everything. Our differences and disagreements melted away as our food settled and the wine warmed us and the moon rose. I still think of that evening now, disconnected from what happened next, a lone, unalterable, perfect moment.

> I still think of that evening now, disconnected from what happened next, a lone, unalterable, perfect moment.

In the movies, there is always a warning when danger approaches, but we woke as though it were any other day. Heather went down to the beach to get beautiful. Peter and I cleaned up camp, took our stuff to the car, and made a second trip to gather what was left. When we got back to the car, not more than a few minutes later, everything was gone.

I remember getting all sweaty and nervous. Maybe Heather had taken everything to the beach to keep it safe? Then we thought everyone who passed had stolen our stuff. Everyone was a suspect—the old man with a cane, the little boy in the Speedo. We didn't make any sense, even to ourselves. We thought maybe Heather had been stolen, too.

Finally, we gave up looking, climbed back into the car, and drove the half-hour to Alicante to file a police report. The officer pointed out the irony of being robbed in a place called The Joyous Village. I didn't think it was funny.

Police reports are hard to do in a foreign language. None of us spoke much Spanish beyond "*¿Dónde está el baño?*" and none of us were able to calculate the exchange rate to value our stuff. I guessed on the high side of Euros, just in case. I was sick with worry.

We also needed to get new passports, so we went back to Barcelona and the U.S. consulate. Our spirits were not high. Peter still had most of his important stuff; he'd kept it with him instead of putting it in the car. (Now I travel with a hip belt, which I take everywhere, even to the shower.) I hate it when being prudent pays off. Peter fooled around Barcelona while Heather and I went to the consulate.

I'd been wearing the same clothes for three days, with no shower, carrying around my remaining belongings in a plastic grocery bag. I expected the U.S. consulate to be a haven for distressed Americans in a foreign land. But the intake clerk made it a challenge from the first moment:

Me: I need a new passport.

Them: We need to see some I.D.

Me: I don't have any I.D. I just got everything stolen.

Them: Do you have a birth certificate?

Me: No. I just got everything stolen.

Them: You know the government suggests that you always keep a photocopy of your birth certificate separate from your passport for cases like these.

Me (my temper rising): Can I speak to someone else? Maybe an *American*?

Them: There is no one else here.

Heather and I managed to provide them with what they needed. We left to eat *churros*, returned to get our new passports, then took the car back to the rental agency in Barcelona. But the location, a note on the door said, had moved. We drove around the city until we found the new place, which meant we delivered the car late, which cost us an extra day's fees. Then they charged us for the damage to the car during the robbery and the gas we'd used driving around the city in search of their new location.

Shortly thereafter, Heather informed us that she was leaving to stay with an ex-boyfriend in Rome. We took her to the airport early the next morning. This is classic, I thought. When things get difficult, the pretty girl goes to stay with some tall, dark, handsome Italian she doesn't even like. (But disasters have a way of bringing people together in the long run: Heather and I are great friends now.)

So Peter and I were left with the wreckage of our

trip. I was feeling tired and low, and I didn't really know what to do. Pete came up with a brilliant solution: We'd take a vacation from our vacation.

We bought two plane tickets to Mallorca. We rented scooters and rode around the whole island. We slept on beaches, met locals, and wore the same clothes every day.

But this time it was good. Each day was its own. Each place was as random as the next. I loved the sun, my scooter, my plastic grocery bag, and travel. I was living like a hobo, and it was the best thing I ever did.

Spain without a backpack isn't the typical travel experience. But that's the great, redeeming quality of travel. Stick with it, and it will show you all these undiscovered corners of yourself—ones you'd never have otherwise known.

ELLIOTT DYKES *is an idealistic, overeducated, career-dodging travel junkie. He has lived abroad eight times and traveled through more than 30 countries on five continents. He has trekked the Himalaya, climbed glaciers in Patagonia, sailed the Mediterranean, seen the Pyramids, given confession at the Vatican, hitchhiked across Israel, bathed in the Ganges, and whiled away many happy days on the beaches of East Asia. He believes in self-development, the value of good people, and work as a statement of purpose. Elliott can be reached at www.chasingeden.com.*

Sevilla

Always Book Ahead

jimmy vielkind

after a six-hour train journey from Valencia to Sevilla, my goal was simple: on a weekend evening at 5 p.m., find a place to stay. Filled with worry as I toted my duffel bag and day pack across the station platform, I decided to take a cab.

Like most cabbies in this world, this fellow didn't quite speak my language. And, even after seven years of studying Spanish, I didn't quite speak his. But I knew enough to ask him to take me to the church of *Santa Maria la Blanca*. My guidebook said there were hostels nearby.

He looked at me quizzically and asked why.

"I'm looking for a bed," I said. "Bed" was much more

in line with my budget than "room." The hostel where I had stayed in Barcelona had offered a bed, along with several other bunks, in a relatively cramped room. My cabbie, however, misunderstood.

"*Se un lugar barato, pero no es tan cerca a la iglesia que quiere,*" he said. I know a cheap place, but it's not as close to the church as you want.

"*¿Es bueno?*" I asked, in a meager attempt to assert standards.

"*¡Es barato!*" was his reply. He weaved in and out of the narrow streets until we reached a white, five-story apartment building, which abutted a larger thoroughfare.

He grabbed my duffel and led me inside, where he called for a woman named Sofia and greeted her with a kiss on the cheek. He explained that I was looking for a bed. I paid him; he heard his radio squawk and sped off.

An old fan swirled near the ceiling, and a dying potted plant sat in the corner by the door. There was no one around, no tourist brochures, no desk—none of the traditional trappings of a hotel or hostel lobby.

"*Deje sus mochillas,*" Sofia said. "*Sube las escalaras conmigo. Le mostro las chicas.*" Leave your bags. Come upstairs with me. I'll show you the girls.

Girls?

Out of the corner of my eye, I noticed a young woman clad only in a towel, walking toward a shower. Around the corner, a stodgy man with a moustache and a crew cut was counting money at a folding card table. "*Estás temprano, pero alguien está aquí.*" You're early, but someone will be around.

It had taken me a few moments, but I finally put it together. The girls upstairs weren't exactly Saint Mary the White. And this was no hostel. It was a brothel. I fumbled through some excuse and rushed out before the burly pimp could shake me down. But once outside, I found myself in the same situation as before—alone in a foreign city with the sun setting fast, carrying bags, and looking for a place to stay. Low on cash and weary of cabbies, I grabbed a map and decided to hoof it.

It was then that I realized that the Spanish and I have different concepts of city planning. I come from New York, where, in 1811, the city fathers carved up Manhattan into a grid that time has proven to be all but idiot-proof. In Sevilla, on the other hand, I was lucky to find a street with a label on it. Checking my map at every corner, I soon found myself walking in circles and still horribly lost, so I started asking every person I passed for directions. They pointed me in more circles, which led me into one-way streets randomly blocked by items such as a massive parade with a 20-foot statue of a saint, and a full marching band.

Two hours and a full tour of the old city later, I found the tiny square with the two hostels named in my guidebook. Both turned out to be full. The manager of the second saw the deflated look on my face, and he told me to follow him across the street. Through a wrought-iron gate and an open courtyard, we entered a building where the air was thick with concrete dust. Scaffolding loomed along the walls. Instead of the metal Hostelling International sign that would mark the place as legitimate, a bad imitation had been stenciled on the wall.

An old man named Manuel came out, looked me from top to bottom, and said, "Twenty." He knew he had landed a customer before I even reached for my wallet. He gave me a key and showed me to a windowless room upstairs. Flies swarmed around the bare bulb that hung from the ceiling. When I dropped my bag, a roach scurried across the floor. I put a T-shirt over the pillow, in a feeble attempt to avoid lice, and collapsed on the bed. It was 9 p.m., four hours after I had arrived at the train station.

Next time, I thought before drifting off, I'll book ahead.

JIMMY VIELKIND *is a student at Columbia University, majoring in urban studies. He has been writing for magazines and newspapers, including the New York Daily News, since graduating from high school. He previously served as city editor of the Columbia Daily Spectator, where he writes a bi-weekly column on urban affairs. He has traveled to Europe several times.*

Sevilla

Meeting Pepe's Mom

miranda runcie

as I walked over the Guadalquivir River on the Puente de las Delicias, I knew I didn't belong. I felt like an *extranjera* with the emphasis on *extraña*—strange. Normally when I tried to appear Spanish (even though everything about me screamed, "Howdy, I'm American!"), I could stand out from other foreigners who surrounded me. But this time I was alone, on my way to meet a Sevillano boy who wanted to introduce me to his family.

I was tired of being an outsider. Masses of people were passing me on the bridge, including those fresh from Sevilla's annual Feria de Abril—the men in spring suits with pastel-pink and baby-blue ties, the women in cascades of rainbow ruffles—and I never once made a gesture of acknowledgement. I wanted to get lost in the mob.

Three months of living in this city had taught me that Sevillano women don't smile at strangers. They always wear sunglasses and usually seem pissed off. To a Midwestern girl who grew up passing people in public with neighborly "hellos," nods, or at least eye contact, these emotionless faces seemed threatening. I wondered what I had done to make them so angry.

No matter how stern my facial expressions, tight my black pants, or pointy the toes of my stilettos, I knew that I was transparently *Americana*. My blonde highlights were like the mark of Cain. Spanish men openly stared and talked at any blonde woman who walked by. At 5-foot-10, I loomed over both sexes just as the magnificent Giralda Tower soared above surrounding buildings in the center of town. Worst of all, I walked confidently, and alone. Spanish women are never alone—if not with a boyfriend or husband, they travel in packs of at least five females.

A dull nervousness throbbed in my gut as I thought of meeting the family. To spite it, I straightened my posture and adjusted my dark glasses. The sun reflecting off the river made my forehead and cheeks burn. I looked off to the water, following a wayward tree branch with my eyes as it floated under the bridge, Mediterranean-bound. The aromas of doughnutty fried *churros* and creamy hot fudge blew toward me as I neared the fair.

Three days before, I had been walking around the fair with my friends Sarah and Emma. A group of friendly older men spotted us. They noticed we weren't locals, but they invited us into their *caseta* anyway, the small, private tents where the fair actually "happens." It was quite an honor, because getting past a doorman requires an invitation. Most non-Sevillanos walk along the streets, trying to get views of the best parties inside the tents. These men were old enough to be our fathers, but their invitation was generous, so we accepted. They made sure to keep our glasses full to the brim with *rebujitos*, the traditional drink of 7-Up mixed with dry sherry, and they let us step on their feet as we performed our own awkward versions of the folk dance *sevillanas*.

Sipping my sherry, I watched from the corner as my friend Emma twirled around the dance floor with a 40-something British ex-pat. Someone scooted past me on his way out of the tent, then stopped with an "*Hola.*" I turned and saw a tall, handsome, 20-something Spanish man. "Where are you from?" he asked me—Germany? England? Norway? When I told him America, his face lit up, and he spoke in English. "Leave these old men and come with me," he said. So I did.

Over the next couple of days and nights at the fair, I managed to spend the majority of my time with him. His name was José Vega Barrera – Pepe for short. He called me *Guapa*, Beautiful, and insisted on paying for all my food and drinks. Putting my feminism aside, I let Pepe pamper me. Maybe I was influenced by movies I'd seen about Spanish lovers. Or maybe it was an adolescent rebellion against my parents' worst fear: "You can go to Spain," my mom had said, "as long as you don't fall in love and stay there forever." I wasn't looking for love, but when Pepe showed up, I decided I had nothing to lose—and maybe a lot to gain.

To me, Sevilla is one of the most romantic cities on Earth. In my few months before Pepe, I had daydreamed of holding hands with someone along the river under the Torre del Oro, toasting sangria over a shared plate of *tortilla española*, and being kissed next to the fountain in the Plaza de España. That was all I asked for: a middle-school romance that was long enough to make a friend and short enough not to make an enemy.

I was surprised then, when Pepe casually asked me to a lunch party to celebrate the last day of the fair. Pepe was hosting the event, and his entire extended family would be there. "Please come. I want everyone to meet you." I suddenly felt scared and bewildered. Wasn't there some sort of Ten Commandments to a Spanish fling? "Thou shalt not meet *la familia* after three days with a boyfriend" had to be near the top of the list. I looked at his face for signs of sarcasm, but saw none.

"Are you sure about this?" I asked. "Yes. Come," he said as he squeezed my hand and shook it playfully. If he was so confident, maybe I should trust him. I closed the car door and bent down to look through the open window. As he rolled it up, he added, "You should know that they don't speak any English." A smirk was the last thing I saw as his car sped away down the narrow road.

After five hours of tossing and turning, I rolled out of bed at 1 p.m., showered and dressed, so I could make the walk across the bridge to the fair by the appointed 3:30 party time. Via several Spanglish cellphone text messages, Pepe had informed me about where to meet him and when, and that he might be a little late because his grandmother was still, as he said, "making herself beautiful."

> I needed to take advantage of every experience, especially if it ripped me out of my comfort zone and stomped on my pride.

On the way to the fair, I considered turning back, but I reminded myself that I was in Spain on an adventure, and that I needed to take advantage of every experience, especially if it ripped me out of my comfort zone and stomped on my pride.

Pepe met me outside his family's *caseta* and led me to where his family sat. His mom, dad, sister, grandma, aunts, uncles and cousins crammed around three round, tea-party-sized tables, and they'd already started their first rounds of beer. Family members taller than 5-foot-7 had trouble getting their knees under the tables.

Pepe introduced me to his dad first. Built like a grizzly bear, he seemed more like a teddy bear when he embraced me. Pepe's grandmother was not the typical petite Spanish woman. She rose to a grand 6 feet, thin and strong—a regal woman. His mom, on the other hand, was very small. Sitting to my right, she wore the traditional flamenco, or *Gitano*, dress, bursting with vibrant reds and yellows, polka dots, and more ruffles than a 1989 senior-prom dress. It was difficult to take anyone dressed like this seriously. Her hair was piled in a bun on top of her head with a gigantic flower attached, and she wore her sunglasses the entire lunch, though no sunlight penetrated the tent's ceiling. She silently critiqued my lack of Spanish-speaking skills. I'm convinced she was thinking, "Pepe, *mi hijo*, why can't you meet a nice Spanish woman?" She intimidated me.

Pepe brought fresh pints of beer to our table. I simultaneously wanted to sip politely for the company and gulp massively to relieve my growing nervousness. My indecision wasn't helped by Grandma and Aunt urging me to drink "*¡más, más!*" All around me, people were leaning toward me, waving their hands and yelling over the lively flamenco music blasting from the speakers. I assumed they were asking me questions or telling me something important, so I nodded, smiled and repeated, "*Sí, sí*" over and over. Like a dog that knows it's being talked to but stares blankly and pants dumbly in response, sounds were all I heard.

I had been studying Spanish all semester, but listening to the Spanish of a teacher who pronounces every sound crisply and clearly is very different from the uninhibited mealtime conversation between family members. When Grandma ran off a riff of sentences and then paused for my reply, all I could do was turn to Pepe, tapping his shoulder frantically. "Help! All I heard was something about a beach and apartment." Everyone seemed concerned that Pepe hadn't taken me to their family's beach house yet. Did they understand that we'd only just met each other? When I turned to his grandmother and said, in my best Spanish, "I likes you...your...uh...elephant" (she was wearing a necklace with an elephant pendant), all conversation ceased. For 10 seconds. Then the tsunami of chatter hit again.

Finally, it was time to eat. Before I saw the food, I recognized the familiar smells of a Spanish kitchen— roasted garlic and olive oil. Eating the food gave me something to do besides stare at the pictures of elderly Gypsy women hanging on the wall.

Pepe was up and down, running from the table to the kitchen, telling the cook what to make for each course. His choices were exquisite. We started with garlic shrimp (emphasis on garlic), *Serrano* ham (similar to Italian prosciutto), tender strips of pork, and potatoes drizzled with olive oil. Our main course was *paella*, the rice dish seasoned with saffron to make it a vibrant golden orange. For dessert, we ate delicate pastries the size of assorted boxed chocolates.

Again, the family urged me to eat and drink more

by pushing second and third helpings in front of me. Wanting to be polite, I smiled and took small bites of everything they offered. The noises kept getting louder and more indecipherable. I realized this event was not slowing down.

Out of the chaos, I heard my name. I turned to my right. Pepe's mother was talking to me. Even though we were sitting next to each other, she hadn't spoken to me since our introduction. I looked at my own reflection in her sunglasses and tried to make out her words. "*Miranda, eres aburrida.*" My mouth dropped and I pointed at myself in disbelief. His mother had just told me, "Miranda, you are boring." I was horrified. Didn't she understand that I was completely alone in this situation, out of my comfort zone, drowning in a vast ocean gasping for breath and flailing my arms? We stared at each other (at least, I think she was looking at me). I didn't know what to say. She repeated herself, but this time I heard it a little differently. "*¿Miranda, estás aburrida?*"

My mind flew back to my first semester of Spanish—the "to be" verbs. It was one of the hardest things about the language. In Spanish, there are two verbs that mean "to be," and depending on which is used, the sentence can have a completely different meaning. *Eres, estás, eres, estás...*ah! My posture relaxed a little once I understood that she had actually asked, "Miranda, *are you* bored?" Relieved, I replied in Spanish, "No. I no bored. I tired. Too much noise. No understand talk."

She nodded and turned back to the conversation she was having with her niece.

I knew she hated me. But what did it matter? I just had to make it through a couple more hours, and then I wouldn't see any of them again. There was no way Pepe was going to call me after this. I wasn't Spanish enough. "Boring American girl," I could just picture them saying after I was gone. For all I knew, they were saying it then, right in front of me. That's what they were really laughing about. I could see it now. Fingers pointing, everyone staring at me with mouths flung open, laughing, mocking, shouting.

"Miranda!" Pepe yelled my name for what was obviously the third or fourth time. I jolted out of my pitiful trance and noticed that the family was leaving the *caseta*. "The coach is here to take all the ladies around the fair. It's our tradition to end the fair this way." He led me outside to a horse-drawn carriage, where the other women sat waiting for me. The only empty spot was on the highest level of seats, alongside Pepe's sister and cousin. Without knowing what to do, I got in and waved goodbye to Pepe. The coach took off for a ride around the fairgrounds.

I felt like I was in a parade—no, *on* parade. Ours was not the only coach, but still everyone was staring at me. I was obviously out of place among these beautiful, very Spanish women. Tourists were taking pictures and pointing and laughing as I rode by. It was humiliating.

But then I noticed something. The women in Pepe's

family were waving and smiling back at the people on the street below. Maybe they *weren't* laughing at me. And maybe they weren't taking my picture to later say, "What the hell was *she* doing with *them*?!" In fact, I realized, no one even noticed me. I was one of them. Sitting high up on a horse-drawn carriage at the fair, everyone assumed I was just another family member. They thought I was Spanish. I sat up straight, smiled wide, and began waving back to children as we passed.

When the ride was over, I climbed off and waited for the other women to get down. I gave them all my "*¡Gracias!*" and said goodbye. Pepe's mom took me aside and, for the first time, lifted her sunglasses onto her forehead. "Tell Pepe," she said in her slowest Spanish, "to give you my phone number so you can call me if you ever need anything." She stretched up toward me and gave me a hug. Then I walked back home confidently, over the bridge.

MIRANDA RUNCIE *received her B.A. in English from Truman State University. She is working on her Spanish and teaching English as a Second Language in Ecuador. Besides writing, traveling and speaking Spanish, her newest passion is playing with her twin nieces, Sydney and Abigail.*

Tarragona to Sevilla

Eight to a Compartment

christine sarkis

When the evening train to Sevilla pulled into our seaside village station at 7:56, we were waiting on the platform. It was early April, and Ruby and I had spent most of the day fruitlessly searching for a stretch of beach warm enough for swimming.

The train's stop was short, so rather than dash down the platform to the correct car, we climbed into the nearest open door. We walked through the narrow passageways of three long cars, dodging the crowds of smokers between carriages and squeezing our tall packs behind people who loitered in the hallways, finally reaching Compartment 7—the one printed on our tickets.

I opened the door and was struck by boisterous laughter. A crowd in animated conversation—I counted eight people—was packed into the eight-person compartment. I shut the door and looked at my ticket, then looked back at the number on the door. This was the right place. I took a deep breath, prepared myself for seat negotiations, and re-opened the door.

Already, a middle-aged couple was getting up, laughing at how 7 and 9 looked almost identical on their tickets. The woman touched my arm as she passed by, laughing again as she headed for Compartment 9; the man cocked his eyebrows at his ticket, pretending to have trouble reading it on his way out. I smiled and mumbled an apologetic *gracias*, feeling guilty for breaking up the party.

Ruby and I swung our backpacks up onto the metal luggage racks that ran the length of the compartment. We both knew the drill for long, overnight train rides: come prepared with books, journals, food, music and light jackets that can double as pillows.

We sat down in the two backward-facing seats that the first couple had left, and then realized we'd put ourselves in the midst of three couples, at least 60 years older than us, all traveling south together. They watched quietly as we settled in and said our *hola*s, then they resumed their laughing and talking.

Our seat mates were small and deeply wrinkled, and, even sitting, it was apparent that none was taller than 5-foot-2. The compartment smelled like old people: cologne from a different era and the faintly sour scent of age. Both the men and the women wore short sleeves, and the folds on their arms and faces were deep and even, etched, I imagined, by a lifetime of bright Spanish sunshine and rough *Ducado* cigarettes.

Almost simultaneously, they all started talking to us. I spoke functional Spanish but struggled to understand them. After failing to make out even basic sentences, I thought they had accents I didn't recognize. Turned out they didn't have teeth. Their dentures would come loose at linguistically important moments, floating to the middle of their mouths, turning, for instance, "*ella piensa*" into "ephapienpha." It would take some getting used to, but with a 12-hour train ride of what was looking to be near-constant conversation, I had plenty of time to adjust.

Little by little, I began to recognize distinct personalities: Maria Cristina, who sat directly across from me, was the ringleader. She spoke the loudest, and she made sure everyone else was participating in the conversation. If they weren't, she would tease them until they jumped back in. Maria Dolores, who sat across from Ruby, was the winker. Whenever she said something to either of us, she would wink mischievously, as if we were all in on a joke. Lola was the quietest of the women, but she had the soft, pretty laugh of a young girl. She and Ruby laughed at the same things every time, and developed a fondness for one another because of it. Maria Cristina's husband, Alfonso, sat next to Ruby and kept offering us cough drops. Maria Dolores' husband, Juan, and Lola's husband were brothers; they looked almost exactly alike. The husbands smoked cigarettes, dozed, and phased in and out of the exchanges on our half of the room.

The women would talk about Ruby and me aloud, then ask us questions. As far as I could figure, it was the same thing shared by grandparents across the globe: the ability to talk simultaneously to a person and about a person to a larger group—the "She's doing very well at school, aren't you dear?" approach.

After two hours in the compartment together, the women had invented entire lives and personalities for us. They decided that Ruby was prettier because she was fatter, and that I was too skinny and needed to start eating meat at least twice a day. I was married, while Ruby had boyfriends in every town, but she would soon have to choose one or risk growing old alone. I was Italian and Ruby was Spanish. However, we were also sisters, the two youngest of six. I was a dancer and Ruby didn't like to work. We listened attentively as they created lives for us. We would veto and add details just as often as they did. It was my idea, for instance, that we were traveling to get jobs as bakers in Sevilla. And Ruby came up with the story that our father had wanted six sons but instead got six daughters, and had made all of us learn to play *futbol* and spit just as if we were boys.

Later, when they felt as if they'd completed our

identities, Maria Cristina asked us who we really were. I think they were slightly disappointed that we were just American students and best friends.

As dusk turned to night, my stomach began growling at a volume that rivaled the noise of the train. I rummaged around in my bag until I found two hard rolls and some loosely wrapped *manchego* cheese with dried-out ends, the center sweating beads of oil. Ruby contributed an apple and three quarters of a chocolate bar. The women watched the preparations of our paltry dinner with indulgent smiles, and the men quietly passed out cans of beer. When we popped them open, they foamed over and we all had to jump forward to catch it all.

> I went out for a walk in the hallway. When I returned, the compartment had been transformed.

After Ruby and I finished everything we had to eat, I went out for a walk in the hallway. When I returned, the compartment had been transformed. The old couples had pushed suitcases together in the middle, making a long serving table, and filled it with bread, cheese, a ham leg, beer and olives. From under seats and inside cases had come the makings of a feast. A bundle resting against the wall under the window held more than a dozen oranges, and Lola's husband unwrapped a sausage that had been sitting on top of a suitcase in the luggage rack. They passed around the ham, cutting pieces directly off the bone, resting the thigh against the side of the suitcase table as they cut their slices. That night I learned that, in Spain, it's just not a party unless there's ham. Everyone heaped their plates with fresh bread and meat and fruit, and the cans of beer kept coming.

The only indications that we were not all gathered around a table at Maria Cristina's house were the rocking of the train and the streaks of light outside the window every time we passed a crossing. To us, a train trip had always meant crappy dining-car fare or some stale rolls. To these old friends, it meant an excuse for a party, hours of eating and laughing and drinking. And by good luck, we got to join in, drinking warm beer and eating soft bread and dense rich olives.

By 2 a.m., everyone was tired and drunk enough to fall asleep for a while. The lights remained low in the compartment, and in the dim light, I saw a grown-up version of those children who play so hard that they fall asleep sitting up. But instead of toys and runny noses, there were dentures peeking out of cardigan pockets, pantyhose pinching at wrinkled knees, slips edging down and skirts riding up, and beer bellies that hung gently over brown-belted trousers. I wanted to tuck them in, but they were all sleeping upright, leaning up against one another, each with a unique snore. I watched them, feeling warm and happy, until I fell asleep. I woke up a few hours later, before dawn. They were chatting and had the ham leg out again.

I never asked them where they were going, or what they were doing. But there was a spirit of adventure among them, whereas I had crossed entire countries without feeling anything more than boredom. These people weren't engaging in travel for travel's sake. They were really going somewhere.

The sun was just rising when I went out to stand in the hallway again. We were speeding through flat farmland. In the distance, the hills glowed orange as the sun crested over them. Back in the compartment, the Marias and Lola squeezed us goodbye and ordered their husbands to collect the bags. They got off the train just after 6 a.m., in a small village where the station was little more than an elevated strip of cracked cement and a ticket booth.

Ruby and I were again two instead of eight. In our suddenly quiet compartment, we found that the couples had left us two oranges and the last beer. It was a little reminder that random seat assignments on a train could land us in the middle of a wonderful new type of travel.

CHRISTINE SARKIS *got her first backpack as a present from a friend who had picked it up at a garage sale. The backpack lasted for 9,458 (air and land) miles before disintegrating into a pile of powdery mildew. Her second backpack, purchased new the following year, has lasted to this day. Sarkis is a contributing editor at SmarterTravel.com.*

Sevilla to Algeciras
Thumbs Up
judy boersema

We were about to break our No. 1 rule regarding hitchhiking: Never split up.

Minutes before, Sally and I had arrived on the outskirts of Sevilla at a perfect hitching spot, approaching the main highway. We assumed our familiar positions. We held out our thumbs in a relaxed, beckoning—but not begging—manner. We gently waved a square of cardboard on which we had written our destination in dark, chunky letters: ALGECIRAS. And we propped our packs against our knees, to better display the Canadian flags adorning them.

In no time at all, a semi-truck approached. The driver made eye contact and pulled his rig over onto the shoulder ahead. Seconds later, another semi-truck pulled up behind us.

Leaving Sally behind with our packs, I dashed ahead and spoke with the driver. Despite my lousy Spanish, I thought I got the gist of what he said. Fernando and his trucking amigo, Diego, in the semi parked behind us, both were headed to Algeciras. Fernando said it was illegal in Spain to have more than one passenger in the cab, but they would be happy to transport the two of us if we would be willing to split up.

I gave Sally the scoop. We debated briefly and decided to go with our thus-far trustworthy gut feelings—we accepted their offer.

Sally and I had begun our trip in London nearly two months earlier. From there, we thumbed our way to Dover and caught the ferry to France. We made our way to Paris, then traveled down through western France and the Loire Valley. We hitchhiked over the border into northern Spain, on through the western and southern coasts of Portugal, and finally back into Spain again. We were planning to stop next on the Costa del Sol and spend a few weeks with a friend.

Our decision to "hitch" was motivated solely by our lack of funds, not by any particular thirst for risk or adventure. And, so far, we had experienced few transportation problems. The weather had been mostly cooperative, and the rides had generally come quickly. As a bonus to the free transportation, in the intimate confines of a vehicle, we felt we were truly getting to know and appreciate Europeans. Our drivers seemed to enjoy the novelty of meeting us, too. They often were downright incredulous at picking up two North American women hitchhiking through their country. The only unpleasant encounters involved the occasional male driver who, after giving us a ride, attempted to say *au revoir, adios* or *adieu* with inappropriately intimate farewell kisses. But, for the most part, we had been treated warmly and respectfully.

Most recently, we had spent two wonderful, relaxing days in gorgeous Sevilla. It was spring, and the city was in full bloom, the air filled with the sweet scent of orange blossoms. We were feeling well-rested and in high spirits on the morning Fernando and Diego rolled up in their semi-trucks.

I climbed into the cab with the young, handsome, mustachioed Fernando. Sally joined the middle-aged, beer-bellied, somewhat smarmy-looking Diego. As we headed off down the road, Fernando and I attempted conversation, but Fernando's English was nearly nonexistent, and my Spanish was limited. I grew weary of trying to converse, and soon we were traveling in silence.

Killing time, I leisurely looked around the interior of the cab. The décor was southern European truck-driver chic: a Saint Christopher medal hung from the rear view mirror; a colorful tasseled banner, imprinted with a likeness of the Virgin Mary, swung breezily from the top of the windshield; affixed to the dash were photos of ample-bosomed women. Sally and I had seen this combination in other Spanish and Portuguese semi-truck cabs.

I switched my attention to the passing scenery. Compared with the lushness of Sevilla, this was quite desolate. Although there were still hints of springtime green in the fields, I imagined that the landscape would soon get predominately brown.

Gazing out at the road ahead and daydreaming, the miles slipped away. When we reached the halfway mark on our journey, we stopped at a roadside café for lunch. Diego followed our lead and pulled up behind us. Despite our protests, Diego and Fernando treated us to tasty ham and eggs, bread, lemonade, coffee and a shot of Quarenta y Tres—a popular Spanish liqueur similar to Grand Marnier. Conversation over the meal was very limited, but good-natured.

> **I was congratulating myself on yet another successful ride.**

Soon we got back on the road, Fernando and me following Diego and Sally. We were only an hour or so from Algeciras, and I was congratulating myself on yet another successful ride—free transport, free food and drink, and a bird's-eye view of the country to boot!

Feeling rejuvenated by lunch, and perhaps a little less inhibited due to the alcohol, I once again attempted to converse with Fernando. I asked about his wife and kids, and I told him about my fiancé in Canada.

Fernando was unable to comprehend how my fiancé would "allow" me to travel without him.

In reality, unlike Sally, I was neither Canadian nor espoused. This was part of my hitching persona. I masqueraded as a Canadian in order to avoid being targeted—or ignored—on the roadside by anti-American Europeans. And the fictional fiancé was supposed to help keep unwanted advances at bay. I was never comfortable with these lies, but they worked, mostly. Many of our drivers said they stopped for us because they'd seen the Canadian flag. It seemed that everyone had a soft spot for the lovable Canadians, and they gushed all over us. Often this was followed by expressions of disdain for Americans, while I sat in silence, squirming with guilt. As for the fictional fiancé, well, Sally and I had found that it did little to deter interested parties from pursuing us.

Once again, the conversation with Fernando died quickly. I gazed out the window. But I soon sensed that Fernando was watching me, so I turned and smiled at him. He returned the smile. Then his gaze began to pass over me, slowly up and down, in a way that made me feel very uncomfortable. I felt the first prickles of fear. He jerked his thumb at the sleeper behind us and made a mostly unintelligible query. Although I didn't understand his exact words, I had a pretty good idea of what he was asking. I played dumb. *"No gracias, no tengo sueno,"* I said. I'm not sleepy. I prayed that would be the end of it.

Meanwhile, I noticed that our semi had fallen so far behind Diego's, they had disappeared from sight altogether. Then, without warning, Fernando turned onto a dirt side road and stopped the truck. I flat-out panicked. I began to shout and curse in English while he spoke in a cajoling tone.

"*Eres muy bonita*," he cooed.

"So what!" I screamed.

He begged, "*Por favor*, Judy," pronouncing my name as if it were spelled "Yoody."

"No, no, no!" I yelled back.

"*¿Por qué no?*" he asked, over and over again.

Somewhere in the back of my mind, it dawned on me that Sally might also be in danger.

"*¿Dónde está mi amiga?*" I asked.

Fernando laughed and said, "*A ella le están dando lo mismo.*" Sally was getting the same treatment.

I had to get out of there. I touched the knife in my pocket, which I often carried "just in case." It was so dull, it could barely cut through a block of cheese, much less inflict any serious damage on a human being. But I was ready to use it if I needed to. I put my hand on the door handle and began to open the passenger door.

Then—I got lucky. Perhaps Fernando was weary of my screeching; perhaps force was never an option in his mind. Maybe he was just hopeful. I don't really know. But he simply sighed deeply and put his hands in the air in a sign of surrender. "Okay, okay, okay," he said. "*Vamos.*"

I closed the truck door as he shifted into reverse and slowly backed onto the highway. He mumbled under his breath the entire way.

As we continued down the highway, I felt incredibly relieved for myself, but sick with worry over Sally. Fernando just shrugged his shoulders when I asked about her. My mind raced. I would need to contact the police in Algeciras as soon as we got there, and perhaps call our friend in the Costa del Sol.

A few miles down the road, we spotted Diego's truck pulled off at a roadside café. Sally was standing alongside the truck, hands on her hips, with a "Where the hell have you been?!" look on her face.

Our truck had barely stopped when I flung the door open and launched myself out of the cab, my arms wrapped tightly around my pack. With the added weight of the pack, I hit the ground so hard it felt as if my legs would drill into the packed soil.

Sally watched my aerial maneuver with her mouth agape. "What happened?" she asked.

"He's an asshole!" was my only reply. And I staggered off to the café. I refused to look back at Fernando, refused to say *"gracias."*

Inside the café, I told Sally the whole frightening story. Diego, it turned out, had been a perfect gentleman. In fact, when Sally noticed that Fernando and I had disappeared from view in her side mirror, Diego seemed to be as concerned as she, and they had pulled over to wait for us.

We meekly took a bus the remaining miles to Algeciras and spent the night in a cheap *pension*, drinking way too much Quarenta y Tres, celebrating my escape from a close call.

The next morning, still feeling a bit apprehensive, we took a bus to the Costa del Sol. Two weeks later, however, we were back on the side of the highway, thumbs in the air. We hitched seven months altogether, through 15 countries, and, in more than 180 rides, nasty incidents were rare. Most notable was another Spaniard, this one certifiably crazy, who wouldn't let us out of his car. He was going to take us to his factory for "a little food, a little 'drinkie,' and a little love."

Together, Sally and I managed to talk our way out of that one. And that's my advice to two women hitchhiking in Europe: Never split up!

JUDY BOERSEMA *lives in the Seattle area and works for a local nursery, where she sells, cares for and writes about plants. She followed up her initial adventures with two solo backpacking trips, traveling via Eurail and visiting an additional 10 countries. She also has traveled to Australia twice to visit Sally, who lives there with her husband and son, and an impressive menagerie of animals.*

Sevilla

Discovering My Duende

elizabeth landau

My flamenco dress has hung in my closet with the same stains for almost two years, but I refuse to clean it. Each splotch and crease reminds me of a different moment from my semester abroad in Sevilla. I hesitate to say "study abroad," because as a young American living there between semesters, studying was not the point of going to Spain—not when the sun sets at 10 p.m. and the streets reawaken with sangria and smoke at 2 a.m.

I went there to become Spanish. Learning the language, I believed, would guide me into a whole world of sensing and seeing, of thinking and behaving, of tradition and history. This turned out to be idealistic.

My plan to make Spanish friends fell through almost immediately when I realized that there was no "campus" at the Universidad de Sevilla, and that outside of class, Spanish students tended to stick with their established groups of friends. Most of my American classmates preferred to speak English most of the time, and friends from other countries faded in and out of my life. I always felt like an outsider and observer, and I wanted to do something to fit in with the Spaniards. So, when my American roommate Sofia suggested dance lessons, I jumped at the chance.

Sevillanas, the flamenco-style folk dance of Sevilla, is danced in four separate routines to the music of a rhythmic, upbeat, guitar-based song. Each routine involves delicately rotating your wrists, taking small but precise steps, and twirling, stomping and exclaiming "¡Olé!" at just the right times.

Sofia and I learned to dance the *sevillanas* from a feisty, unpleasant-smelling, impatient blonde Spaniard named Nuria, whose pudgy body took up most of the space in her living room. My lack of coordination did not help as she demonstrated the four movements for us. When I forgot one part of a routine and mistakenly stepped forward with my right foot several times, she slapped my left thigh and ordered "¡La izquierda!" I was also reluctant to dance near to her, which irked her, because *sevillanas* is a close-in partner dance.

I'd just about finished with Nuria when she took us to a dress shop around the corner from her house. That was when I saw *the dress*, black with large white polka dots. Flamenco dresses are made of layers of taffeta extending to the floor, which puff out at the bottom as the dancer twirls in circles, faster and faster. I'll never forget going into the cluttered dressing room and zipping up the long skirt, then slipping on the matching blouse and jacket. I had by then spent three months in Spain, feeling too white, too American. Suddenly, this dress connected me to Spain; it gave me style and purpose.

When Feria de Abril arrived—one week straight of dancing and drinking after a rest from Easter celebrations—my American friends and I proudly walked across the San Telmo Bridge wearing tap shoes, *trajes de flamenco*, and flowers in our hair, just like thousands of Spanish women around us. At the Feria festival, there are hundreds of striped tents with a different party in each. When people want a break from dancing and drinking, they come outside to play carnival games or ride the Ferris wheel. All day, horse-drawn wagons carry men and women, their feet and skirts hanging off the sides. At all hours of the night, people sing about the dance queen of the Triana or Macarena districts, and they dance the four *sevillanas*. I understood that this dance would be my ticket into the Spanish world, as long as I kept my feet going, returning to Feria each day in my dress.

> **Suddenly, this dress connected me to Spain; it gave me style and purpose.**

For sure, I was one of the clumsiest dancers there. I tripped on my skirt several times, as the dust on the skirt's bottom ruffles reveal. Nuria had failed to teach me the hand movements for two entire dance segments, so I had no idea what to do after the 360-degree turn on the third movement, or during the entire fourth part. But I had the basic vocabulary in my heels, in my mind, and on my lips. I could go up to anyone—old or young, male or female—and ask to dance. And, just as I had expected, I met Spaniards from all over Spain, improving a different step of my dance with each new encounter.

All week, I watched dancers rotate their hips, stomp their feet, and circle their wrists with startling precision. Confident and passionate, they possessed *duende*, that indefinable force and spirit that propels much of Spanish art and motion. I was jealous when even a 7-year-old girl outdanced me, and I laughed when I got confused on the third movement. Her movements were as spotless as her blue dress. My dress had already collected splotches from the puddles at the foot of the bridge, where a German and a Cypriot carried Sofia and me on their backs, and near the bar where Sofia and I had long conversations in Spanish about injustices and politics, where I first learned to speak the lyrical Spanish of an Argentine.

When I look at my dress now, I realize that I wouldn't trade my smattering of international encounters in it for anything. That was my "study" in Spain. I think of the city's motto, "NoDo," which stands for "*Sevilla no me ha dejado.*" It means "Sevilla has not left me." A dirty flamenco dress I haven't worn since April 2004 reminds me that it's true.

ELIZABETH LANDAU *still cannot properly dance sevillianas, but she would love to one day go back to Sevilla and learn how. She now attends Columbia University's Graduate School of Journalism, and she hopes to become a writer.*

Sevilla to Cadiz
A Bang-Up Job
lauren trojniar

When three acquaintances from my study-abroad program invited me to road-trip from Granada through Sevilla to the city of Cadiz, I quickly accepted. It was a beautiful spring, we were short on holiday time, and renting a car was cheaper and faster than the lazy southern bus. They asked if I could drive a manual transmission—the cars in our price range were manuals—and I told them I could, kind of. I didn't tell them I had done well in parking lots. When I learned that one of the girls, Lacy, borrowed her brother's manual all the time, my stomach settled back down.

The car rental was a good deal: We would pay some ridiculously low rate for five days of use, and we could drop it off in Cadiz, where we were to meet up with the rest of our group. All we had to do was return the car with a full tank of gas and in the same condition in which we received it.

We started early the following afternoon, on a clear blue Granadan day. Our car was cute. It didn't look like something you'd drive; it looked like something you'd pedal. Our trusty driver turned the key, and we lurched forward. She stalled once—okay. She stalled again—unfamiliar car. The third time—nerves. My other friends and I were silent, as if even our breathing could startle the car.

The fourth try got us out of the lot and headed toward a one-way, steep cobblestone path that was littered with tourists. This was the wrong way. We would have to find someplace wide enough to turn around. A slow scrape along the side of the car brought us to another stop. We all jumped out to look at minor damage from a stone block.

"Will you drive?" came Lacy's quiet request.

I sat in the driver's seat, wrestled with the gear shift, and found reverse gear eluding me, so my only option was forward. We didn't have a map of this section of Granada, Sacramonte, as we hadn't intended to drive the winding gypsy roads. But we made it to the open highway and to the outskirts of legendary Sevilla in only a few hours.

We had no plan. We would go where the road took us, find some charming hotel, and party the night away with the locals. With no stops and no traffic, I gained some confidence.

Once in Sevilla, however, the main road became a one-way street without warning. The next road we turned onto was so narrow that our mirrors scraped the sides of the orange and yellow buildings. We came to a fork, hesitated, and realized we had to go left—a matter of making a "k" turn in the center of a narrow intersection. This, of course, meant reversing. A storefront ahead of us with a huge, glass window displayed large, colorful lamps. I couldn't find reverse. Shouldn't it be obvious? Was there a magical reverse switch I didn't know about? My friends, the traffic director, the store owner and I watched with horror as I inched toward the glass in my effort to reverse.

> I couldn't find reverse. Shouldn't it be obvious? Was there a magical reverse switch I didn't know about?

Cars were honking and the traffic director was waving us to stop, but ... we went straight into the store. The window shook with a tremor and sent the owner out to yell. A passerby hurried to our aid, demonstrating how to push a button in the middle of the shifter to reverse. Thanking him profusely, we peeled out, laughing.

I parked on the sidewalk, as I had seen other small cars do, and we found a hotel. It wasn't charming, but the owner was able to direct us to a parking garage that would be much safer than the sidewalk.

The next morning brought me back to the driver's

seat. After our minor accidents, Lacy was too terrified to try driving again. We surveyed the damage. There were several long, white scratches on the front of the car, light scratches on the left side, and minor damage to both side mirrors. It was about an hour's journey to Cadiz—plenty of time to brainstorm our way out of paying for this.

One idea was to buy nail polish in the same shade as our car, but green was hard enough to find; forget about mint green. We thought about not saying anything until they asked, and then telling them that the scratches were there when we got the car. But the solution that sounded best was to cover up everything with mud. If we could just go off-roading for a bit, mud splatters would cover the damage. The problem was that southern Spain hadn't seen rain in weeks. Still debating, we reached Cadiz with an hour before we had to meet the group. Now that we were in a city, finding even a mud puddle seemed impossible—unless, of course, we made one ourselves.

We parked the car and walked to one of the city's main plazas. One person stood guard, one person held open a plastic sandwich bag, one person borrowed dirt from a potted plant, and the last person mixed in the water. We scrambled back to the car and debated the "natural look of a mud splatter." Some mud we wiped directly on the car, but most of it we flicked on at an upward angle from behind the wheels. Over the mirrors, over the sides, over the front end, even under the car.

Just before our hour was up, we dropped off the car and key, no questions asked. Mud still under our fingernails, we took off with a good story to laugh about for the rest of our semester in Spain.

LAUREN TROJNIAR *is a preschool teacher from Austin, Texas. She now owns a manual transmission.*

Granada

The Curse of the Tasseled Loafers

peter j. malcolm

they were good shoes. Sleek, black, leather loafers with tassels sitting proudly below the tongues. They produced a satisfying "smack!" with each footstep. These shoes were made to be worn to theme music—Saturday Night Fever theme music. Good shoes, indeed. But on a balmy late summer evening in the heart of Granada, *mis zapatos* became more than mere accessories. They became a size-10½ curse.

I was studying with a group of American students in Alicante, and I'd come to Granada with them for the weekend. We'd done our day of cultural enrichment—most notably, touring the 14th-century Moorish castle

Alhambra—and, come nightfall, our group of 18- to 22-year-olds was ready to experience some of the city's more modern pleasures.

At 8 p.m., the troops were assembled and we stormed the city, twenty-odd college students halfway around the world, seeking refuge in an atmospheric Irish pub. Drinks were served, and by 10 p.m., we were belting out Elton John songs and pledging our undying love to each other.

The next stop, it somehow was decided, would be *Granada 10*, an old theater-turned-nightclub that apparently was one of the city's best nightspots. An eavesdropping local man offered to take us to the club—ostensibly a polite Spaniard helping some confused foreigners, but more likely an opportunist trying to keep company with our bevy of American beauties. Regardless, we were thankful for his services, as some among us couldn't find the bathroom without assistance.

After what seemed like an eternity of walking (being mindful not to scuff my footwear), we arrived at our destination, a grand building nestled somewhere within the maze of the city. While most of the group joined the line snaking along the sidewalk, I waited for a few of the stragglers, relishing a moment of peace.

I was puffing away on a Marlboro, thinking about how glorious my current situation was, when I was jolted out of my tranquility by some of my buddies who had left the front of the line.

"Yo, Pete, let me borrow your shoes," interrupted Fat John (who, ironically, is quite slender). "They won't let me in with my tennis shoes."

The three other guys with Fat John were in the same predicament. The plan they devised was to take turns using my exquisite footwear to enter the club, whereupon the shoes would be relayed back to the next in line.

It all sounded fine to me. I mean, how could someone wearing such finely crafted *zapatos* be selfish with them? So, I slipped off the loafers, handed them to Fat John with a slight pang in my chest, and stood in my socks as he stumbled back to the entrance.

> I mean, how could someone wearing such finely crafted *zapatos* be selfish with them?

The first exchange went smoothly. The bouncer admitted Fat John, who handed the shoes off to Agron at the far end of the outdoor patio. Agron's entrance was equally uneventful, and I watched with satisfaction as my shoes were turned into an all-access pass, allowing the possessor to enter even the most tightly restricted areas. Next up was Brad, and then Dave; both slipped into the club unquestioned and made a smooth and, by all accounts, unnoticed handoff.

After getting passed around like a basketball at a Globetrotter's game, the footwear was returned to its true owner. I slipped on the shoes, trying hard not to notice their new steaminess, and walked back to join the line. Looking past the bouncer, I saw Fat John teetering from the club out onto the patio, in his tired-looking Adidas footwear, bouncing to the thumping bass from inside.

"Dude, this club is so tight!" he hollered.

Perfect timing. I had come to the head of the line and had my money and ID ready. The only thing standing between me and said club was an imposing walkie-talkie-wielding Spaniard on a power trip. The bouncer, probably perturbed by the influx of rambunctious travelers from the other side of the pond, simply shook his head.

"*No peudes entrar,*" he said cooly. "*Los zapatos no son el tuyo.*"

I was by no means fluent in Spanish—in fact, I'd been studying it for only 10 days and could barely order a beer—but I knew something was wrong when the velvet rope stayed clipped and the gatekeeper moved on to other clientele. Apparently, the bouncer thought I was borrowing somebody else's shoes.

"I swear, these are my shoes; I just let my friends borrow them. Can you please let me in?" I pleaded.

As far as the bouncer was concerned, I could have been yelling the recipe for a Danish meatloaf. He didn't understand me; if he did, he certainly didn't seem to care.

So there I was, fuzzy-brained and alone, unable to comprehend how such a promising evening had become derailed in such an aggravating manner. I flagged down the first cab I saw, gave the bouncer my best attempt at an intimidating glare, and was whisked back to my hotel, lively flamenco music mocking me from the rear speakers.

By the time I arrived back at my room, my rage had subsided. I sat on the bed and stared at the shoes that had caused me so much grief during this memorable evening.

Tonight they did me no good, but I couldn't stay mad at them. I mean, the shoes were just too good. Too good, indeed.

PETER J. MALCOLM *received a journalism degree from Western Washington University. He is yearning to return to Granada, where he plans to bring his magic loafers and enter the forbidden realm of Granada 10. His story "My First Year in Spain" appeared in "Europe From a Backpack."*

Granada
Goodbye, Granada
katherine lent

I couldn't shake the feeling that I was not ready to leave Spain. As I sat reflecting with my closest friends on our past three-and-a-half months in Granada, we couldn't believe how much we had packed in, or how much we had grown. We joked about how we had dreamed of flings with Spanish lovers. We had not found them, yet we knew we had fallen in love. The city of Granada had stolen our hearts and a bit of our innocence. And while we had shed some tears during difficult times, they would not compare to the tears we'd cry when we finally had to say goodbye.

When I arrived in Granada, the city took my breath away. The Alhambra loomed over the city, the

Christopher Columbus statue shone in the afternoon sun, and the arid Sierra Nevada mountains baked in the Andalusian heat. I felt blessed that I would be able to call this city my home for the next few months. Living and studying abroad had been a dream of mine since high school. So, as the end of my junior year in college approached, I couldn't wait to spend the summer exploring a new country.

Now, as my friends and I reviewed our adventures, we were surprised by where they had led us—as far away as Rabat, Morocco, and as nearby as Madrid, where I ran into a high-school friend in our hostel room. But we all agreed that our best memories were of Granada, and the little things of everyday life.

My daily routine gave me great pleasure, because it meant that I had truly found a home here. Early each morning, I walked 30 minutes into town for class, which even on the coldest morning could be the most refreshing part of my day.

Most shops had not yet opened, but delicious aromas came from the *croissanteria*. An old man was always setting up his used-furniture shop, a collection that never seemed to change. On the next block of Calle Elvira was the elderly woman who clutched her tiny dog as she leaned out her window to swap stories with a neighbor. Three floors up, a stern, grumpy man smoked his morning cigarette while his dog growled at pedestrians on the street below. In Plaza Nueva, dogs basked in the sun while their owners chatted on benches, enjoying the fresh morning air. Sometimes I would stop at the small shop by our program center for a bottle of water and a chat with the kind man who always seemed so interested in my time in Granada.

After morning classes, my friends and I followed the Spanish custom of eating a second breakfast in one of the bustling cafés—usually *tostadas* and *café con leche* at Café Central, which was filled with locals and cigarette smoke. Occasionally, colorful Calle Elvira characters came to start their day with a local Alhambra beer or glass of whiskey. We certainly didn't come to the café for the service: Although we ate there literally every day, the waiters consistently acted as though they had never seen us before. Our program director laughingly referred to us as "*masoquistas*," but we kept going back.

No matter what we ended up doing for the rest of the day, the best part was running across the bohemian characters in this small city. There was the recorder-playing man who appeared in different plazas. There was the British man we nicknamed Stonehenge, after he told us he came from a "magical place" near the famous ruins, and the Irish man we nicknamed Phinneus O'Finnery. Both had come to Granada on "permanent vacations" in their teens, and they now sat on street corners, strumming their guitars and bumming cigarettes off passersby. Downtown, from blocks away, we could hear the American who played his keyboard and belted out songs over his microphone. The "Caveman," who lived in the Gypsy homes of Sacramonte, told us that life in a cave without electricity was the way to go. Another of our favorites was the "man with the smallest dog in the world." He was an aggressive-looking Granadino with shaggy, unkempt hair and big silver necklaces, but he was always kind and compassionate with his tiny dog.

These people became part of our daily lives.

Taking part in another Spanish tradition, we spent our evenings in bars. Granada is the only city in Spain that serves free tapas with drinks, and we took full advantage of this. Hidden behind the statue of Christopher Columbus and Queen Isabel was a bar whose name we could never remember; we called it "the good place." We also were regulars at Antiguana on Calle Elvira near Plaza Nueva, a medieval-looking bar that would get so packed, people would have to bring their drinks outside. The Chilean bartender always greeted us with hugs and kisses, whether he saw us at the bar or around town.

On the other hand, there was nowhere we stood out more than at Café Elvira, where every person had dreadlocks, multiple piercings and a dog by their side. But we loved the atmosphere, the walls covered with pictures of regulars, and the names scratched into the tables and barstools. And Café Elvira served some of the best tapas in town.

As the temperatures dropped and the Sierra

Nevadas became covered in snow, we saw less of our street-dwelling friends Phinneus and Stonehenge. On one of our last days, we saw them in the distance, huddled under blankets and looking fragile in the bitter cold. On our last night as regulars in "the good place," our chubby bartender with the dark sunglasses served us free shots "for the road."

On our last morning in the city, we enjoyed our usual meals at Café Central, trying to keep from getting too sentimental. We couldn't help laughing at the fact that leaving this place meant so much to us, while the waiters seemed never to have noticed us in the first place. We inhaled the last whiffs of cigarette smoke and roasting coffee, said *adios* to our waiter, and whispered our own goodbyes to this café that had become a place we could call our own.

The morning I left the city, I took a taxi to the bus station. It passed so many places I had come to know and love that I couldn't help but finally let my tears out. When the taxi dropped me off, I saw that my three friends were puffy-eyed, too. I couldn't believe our summer was over. As the bus pulled away and out of the city, I knew the words of poet Francisco de Icaza were true: "There is nothing like the pity of being blind in Granada."

KATHERINE LENT *is a senior at Santa Clara University, majoring in communications and Spanish. She hopes for a career with many opportunities to travel. She is from Bellevue, Washington.*

acknowledgements

Muchas gracias to our contributing writers, including those whose work did not appear in this book, for brilliantly capturing the experience of traveling around Spain; to our readers and fellow travelers, who purchased the first book, *Europe From a Backpack*, and thus made the one in your hands possible; to our friends and family for sharing our excitement for these stories; to booksellers who love what they do and put our books face out in their travel sections; and to the people of Spain, for Jamon Iberico and siestas.

about the editors

MARK PEARSON founded Pearson Venture Group after graduating from the University of Washington with a degree in business. After studying art history in Rome and backpacking around Europe for four weeks, Mark decided to compile a collection of the best backpacking stories he could find. So, he created the Europe From a Backpack series (www.europebackpack.com). Also, as the publisher of Dennis Bakke's national bestseller, *Joy at Work: A Revolutionary Approach to Fun on the Job* (www.dennisbakke.com), he recommends you pick up a copy of that book, too. He lives and works in Seattle, Washington.

mark@europebackpack.com

MARTIN WESTERMAN, who has lived in and backpacked around Europe, is the author of *How to Flirt, Easy Green, The Business Environmental Handbook* and hundreds of articles. He lectures on communications and sustainable business practices for the University of Washington Business School in Seattle, Washington, where he lives with his wife, two sons, and edible garden.

martin@europebackpack.com

TRACY CUTCHLOW has traveled in Europe, China, New Zealand, Central America, the U.S. and Mexico. Backpacking is her favorite way to go. After working as a copy editor at The Oregonian, The Capital Times and The Seattle Times, she now produces special projects for seattletimes.com. She has edited several travel and business books. She lives in Seattle, Washington.

tcutchlow@gmail.com

other books in the series

Italy From a Backpack

Dive into Italy with these fresh storytellers, and ...

• Sneak past Vatican guards to see Michaelangelo's Pietà

• Break out of a locked hostel to catch the train to Rome

• Find a surprise romance in Cinque Terre's fresh sea air

• Meet your cheek-pinching, food-loving Sicilian relatives in the old country.

Europe From a Backpack

Feel your love for travel come alive with 58 fantastic backpacking stories from Spain, Italy, France, Germany, Switzerland, Austria and more!

• Billy Anderson stares down death in Pamplona, Spain

• Lisa Cordeiro takes a will-work-for-food approach to travel as a waitress at a Parisian restaurant

• And Mike Riley's desperate search for underwear in a Portuguese market...well, that's another story.

To learn more about hostels, Eurail passes, study-abroad programs and tours, visit www.EuropeBackpack.com